The Healthy Hedonist Holidays

A Year of Multicultural, Vegetarian-Friendly Holiday Feasts

MYRA KORNFELD

ILLUSTRATED BY SHEILA HAMANAKA

SIMON & SCHUSTER PAPERBACKS   New York • London • Toronto • Sydney

SIMON & SCHUSTER PAPERBACKS
1230 Avenue of the Americas
New York, NY 10020

First Simon & Schuster trade paperback edition October 2007

SIMON & SCHUSTER PAPERBACKS and colophon are registered trademarks
of Simon & Schuster, Inc.

For information about special discounts for bulk purchases,
please contact Simon & Schuster Special Sales at
1-800-456-6798 or business@simonandschuster.com.

Designed by Dana Sloan

Manufactured in the United States of America

10   9   8   7   6   5   4   3   2   1

Library of Congress Cataloging-in-Publication Data
Kornfeld, Myra.
    The healthy hedonist holidays : a year of multicultural, vegetarian-friendly
holiday feasts / Myra Kornfeld ; drawings by Sheila Hamanaka.
        p.   cm.
    Includes index.
    1. Cookery.   2. Vegetarian cookery.   3. Cookery, International.   4. Menus.
I. Title.
TX714.K655 2007
641.5'68—dc22   2007027830

ISBN-13: 978-0-7432-8725-8
ISBN-10:   0-7432-8725-8

Acknowledgments

A BOOK IS ALWAYS a team effort, and I am so grateful for the generosity, love, and support of many people without whom this book would not be possible.

A heartfelt thanks to everyone at Simon & Schuster, especially to editor Sydny Miner for entrusting me with this joyful project. My warmest thanks to Dana Sloan for such a beautiful interior design and layout.

Thanks to everyone who graciously tested all the recipes and offered excellent suggestions. Thank you to Derek Treur, who helped get the testing off the ground, and to Jennifer Brawn, who beautifully wrapped up the testing and who gave me the idea of rolling the pesto in the flounder. Special thanks to excellent Russell Lehrer, whose competence and feedback in testing continues to be so valued and appreciated, and who kindly shared the nifty salmon-rolling technique with me. Thanks to Alison Dearborne Rieder for introducing me to cabbage sauerkraut pierogis and for teaching me the dragon fold. I'm grateful to Jean Anderson for sharing her family recipe for deliciously tender pierogi dough.

So much love goes to my dear friend Glynnis Osher for her unwavering support and for going to extra lengths to make the cover so lush and festive. A special thanks to Sheila Hamanaka for such beautiful and illuminating food drawings. I am forever grateful to my dear friend Linda Erman for her enthusiastic and loving presence, and for capably assisting me in hours of painstaking research and editing.

The Natural Gourmet Cookery School in New York City deserves special acknowledgment for being such a vital center devoted to good and healthy food; a special thanks to founder Annemarie Colbin for continuing to be an inspiration, and to director Jenny Matheau for the opportunity to teach and share and learn so much from my students; thanks to my students, who are forever a source of motivation.

A special word of gratitude to the following people: to Melanie Jackson for being such an intelligent and terrific agent; to Clara Rosamarda, who gives me great advice at just the right moments; to Frances Gozland for broadening my cultural horizons.

I am truly blessed to have such unflaggingly supportive and loving parents, Charlotte and Irving Kornfeld, as well as exceptionally loving and generous in-laws, David and Arlene Massimilla.

My deepest appreciation goes to my dear husband, Stephen, who offers essential editorial and gustatory feedback, and who is a source of love and joy in my life.

To the Massimillas, with gratitude

Contents

Introduction

THE HEALTHY HEDONIST HOLIDAYS: *A Year of Multicultural, Vegetarian-Friendly Holiday Feasts* includes feasts for many holidays that Americans of different heritages, ethnicities, and religions celebrate; included are Ramadan, Thanksgiving, Chanukah, Christmas Eve, Christmas Day, Kwanzaa, New Year's Eve, New Year's Day, Chinese New Year, Valentine's Day, St. Patrick's Day, Passover, Easter, Cinco de Mayo, and the Fourth of July. The lavish menus in this book fall under the category of "flexitarian": Each features recipes for a vegetarian main course, as well as either a fish or a poultry entrée; you can make them both, or one without the other. There's a plan for the entire meal from starter to dessert, including salads, soups, sides, and splashes. Dishes in the ensemble go together like a coordinated wardrobe; you can pull together any or all for a variety of combinations.

Holidays are times when we have an opportunity to stop the normal hustle and bustle of our everyday pace; they punctuate the rhythm of the year and mark the cycles of our lives. These celebrations are constantly evolving, and the meanings we ascribe to them today are sometimes quite different from the significance we attributed to them in the past. Our personal relationship with a specific holiday may have changed too; the way we once celebrated it or the foods we once consumed on that holiday may no longer be appropriate. Often our guests may have conflicting food requirements. Whenever I have a dinner party, I find a variety of types of eaters at the table. One person eats fish and vegetarian, another omnivore can't tolerate dairy, and yet another is allergic to beans or sugar. I quickly learned that when my guests are accommodated, they feel especially grateful and welcome.

Many of us have had the experience of finishing an indulgent meal only to feel heavy,

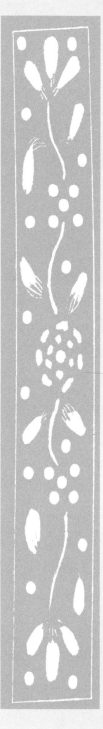

stuffed, and guilty shortly thereafter. These holiday feasts, which are naturally healthy and satisfying, are designed to leave us feeling energetic and nourished *after* the meal as well as delighted during the experience. The individual recipes are bright and flavorful, with an abundance of scrumptious vegetable dishes. Whole grains are used when suitable, although some unbleached flour is the appropriate choice in traditional fare such as pierogis and gnocchi. The majority of desserts include whole grain flours when they do not compromise flavor. I make use of high-quality fats, natural sugars, and the best of each season's produce.

In America, we are privileged to have a multicultural, multiethnic society, and the recipes in this book pay tribute to our culinary smorgasbord. Many of the menus have ethnic spins or contemporary twists to them. For Christmas Eve, I've chosen an Eastern European, mostly Polish-inspired menu. Thanksgiving has a southwestern flair, Kwanzaa features an Ethiopian-style feast, and Easter pays homage to Greek traditions. The lasagna from Christmas Day includes squash and portobello mushrooms, the cranberry sauce from Thanksgiving is brightened with persimmons, and the matzo ball soup for Passover has herbed matzo balls floating in a vibrant green spinach base. The traditional gefilte fish is transformed into an herbed fish loaf studded with seasonal asparagus.

With fragrant scents wafting through the kitchen, you can use your stove as a means of transport to worlds apart from your own when you have feasts in honor of the traditions of others. Even if you are not Chinese, how celebratory it is to have a Chinese New Year's feast, and what an opportunity to learn more about the festival. You may not be Jewish, but what fun it is to have a latke party. Or perhaps the way you celebrate a familiar holiday needs to be refreshed. Your heritage may not be Polish or Ukrainian, but you may be inspired to try pierogis on Christmas Eve for a delicious change of pace.

You can cook the entire group of recipes for each feast or you can choose a selection depending on your needs. If you're making only four or five dishes, the recipes serve six. If you make the entire menu, you will most likely find yourself with enough food for ten or twelve. The dishes all scale up well for large gatherings. I've included a suggested timeline for each entire menu so that you can pace the cooking, the key to an enjoyable experience. Festive occasions are opportunities to go all out and put in a little more effort than usual, but it's no blessing to become exhausted cooking for a holiday. How ironic to celebrate a holiday, with the theme of freedom, renewal, or independence, only to end up too fatigued to enjoy the festivities! If you spread the cooking out over several days, the complete menu comes together relatively effortlessly. All the menus have quite a few dishes or parts of dishes that can be made well ahead, and I have made notes on which dishes freeze well. If you need chiles for Cinco de Mayo or fermented black beans for the Chinese New Year, for instance, purchase them ahead of time. If the ingredients are not at a convenient store near where you live, mail-order them. I've included a resource list (page 251) for anything potentially difficult to find; it usually takes only a few days to arrive on your doorstep.

These feasts make great seasonal dinner party fare. Have a midwinter get-together with the menu from Valentine's Day. Celebrate birthdays with the Moroccan-inspired menu from Ramadan or the Italian-inspired one from New Year's Eve. Or pick a single dish and build a simple meal around the centerpiece for weeknight meals. Keep the gnocchi from New Year's Eve and the chickpea strudel from Ramadan in your freezer, ready to cook up for an impromptu meal. Why not treat every day as a holiday? Many of these dishes travel well. Try the Three Sisters Polenta Casserole or the Black Bean and Plantain–Stuffed Peppers if you're contributing the vegetarian entrée for Thanksgiving, or try the Mushroom Tart with Parmesan Crust from the New Year's Eve menu to bring to an office party.

Party cooking, to me, is the most enjoyable type of cooking there is. The dishes are satisfying to prepare, with the resulting effort bringing moans of appreciation at the table. Infuse your food with intention and cook joyfully. Savor the cooking process as an integral part of the celebration. You create the sacred space necessary for the holiday to be a deeply nourishing experience.

Stocks

To make your food especially flavorful, extend just a little extra effort and make a stock or purchase one from a market that makes their own fresh. Homemade stocks are not labor-intensive, and the resulting depth of flavor is difficult to attain from the packaged varieties. Stock can be prepared well in advance and then frozen.

Here are three of my favorite stocks, a deeply rich roasted vegetable version that is delicious with the winter soups, a chicken stock make from gelatin-rich wings, and an all-purpose vegetable.

Roasted Root Vegetable Stock

The finished brew is so flavorful it's worth the extra effort it takes to roast the vegetables. Lightly salt the stock to turn it into a tasty broth.

MAKES 7 CUPS

2 large leeks, green and white parts, washed and cut into 1-inch pieces
½ pound carrots, peeled and cut into 1-inch rough cut (3 medium, 1 heaping cup)
¾ pound parsnips, peeled and cut into 1-inch rough cut (2½ cups)
1 pound celery root, peeled and cut into 1-inch chunks (4 cups)
2 medium onions, roughly chopped (2 cups)
½ pound sweet potatoes, peeled and cut into 1-inch cubes (2 cups)
2 tablespoons extra virgin olive oil
1 teaspoon salt
2 bay leaves
Handful of fresh thyme (bunch size of a dime in diameter)
Handful of parsley leaves and stems
12 cups water

Preheat the oven to 400°F. In a large bowl, toss the leeks, carrots, parsnips, celery root, onions, and sweet potatoes with the oil and salt. Line 2 baking trays (1 standard size and 1 small will do), spread the vegetables on the trays, and roast for 40 minutes, stirring once or twice, until the vegetables are tender and browned.

Pour the vegetables into a large (6- to 8-quart) pot and add the bay leaves, thyme, parsley, and water. Bring the liquid to a boil, uncovered. Lower the heat and simmer 45 minutes to an hour until the broth is flavorful. Strain the broth, pushing the solids against the side of a strainer to release all of the liquid. You should have about 7 cups of liquid. Use right away, or store in the refrigerator for up to a week and in the freezer for up to a couple of months.

Roasted Chicken Wing Stock

Chicken wings have lots of gelatin in them, so your stock will be gel-like when cooled.

MAKES 8 TO 9 CUPS

Salt
3 pounds chicken wings
2 leeks, green and white parts, washed and cut into 1-inch pieces
2 medium onions, roughly chopped (2 cups)
2 carrots, peeled and roughly chopped (⅔ cup)
2 celery stalks, roughly chopped (1 heaping cup)
4 garlic cloves, unpeeled, halved
About 6 thyme sprigs
About 6 parsley stems
1 teaspoon black peppercorns
1 bay leaf
12 cups water

Preheat the oven to 400°F and line a large baking sheet with parchment paper.

Lightly salt the chicken wings and place on a rack over the prepared baking sheet. Roast for 30 to 45 minutes, until tender and golden. Remove from the oven and let cool a few minutes. Pull the meat off the thick part of the wings and reserve for another purpose. Add the wings to a stockpot along with the remaining ingredients. Bring to a boil, uncovered, lower the heat, and simmer for 1 1/2 to 2 hours, until the stock is flavorful. Strain, pushing the solids against a strainer to extract as much liquid as possible. Use right away, or cool to room temperature and store in the refrigerator for up to 4 days or freeze for several months.

All-purpose Vegetable Stock

This is a good all-purpose stock. The shredded romaine lends a flavorful touch.

MAKES 7 TO 8 CUPS

2 tablespoons extra virgin olive oil
3 cups leek greens, washed and chopped into 1-inch pieces
2 medium onions, roughly chopped
2 stalks celery, roughly chopped
2 carrots, peeled and roughly chopped
4 garlic cloves, unpeeled, halved
1 medium sweet potato, roughly chopped
1/4 pound green beans
1/2 cup white wine
10 cups water
About 6 thyme sprigs
About 6 parsley stems
1/2 teaspoon black peppercorns
1 head romaine, shredded
1 bay leaf

Warm the olive oil in a stockpot or large pot over medium heat. Add the leek greens, onions, celery, carrots, garlic, sweet potato, and green beans and sweat for 10 minutes. Add the wine and cook for 5 minutes until reduced by half. Add the water, thyme, parsley, peppercorns, lettuce, and bay leaf. Bring the liquid to a boil, uncovered. Lower the heat and simmer 45 minutes to an hour, until the flavor has developed. Strain, pressing against the strainer to extract as much liquid as possible. Use right away, or cool to room temperature and store in the refrigerator for up to 5 days or freeze for up to 2 months.

Ingredients

These menus are seasonal, designed for produce that is at the height of flavor. For the best results, use the freshest ingredients available. Although I am a hearty advocate of organic eating, I opt for locally raised produce over organic that is shipped long distances. Visit a local greenmarket for the best local just-picked varieties of fruits and vegetables. The healthiest and best-tasting eggs, dairy, poultry, and meat come from animals raised traditionally, humanely, and organically. Whenever possible, I like to meet the growers producing the food I purchase so that I can inquire about their farming methods. I buy my eggs and dairy, for instance, from Abner Lapp and Mark Nolt, two Amish farmers who have their products delivered regularly to New York City. Their chickens are free to run around and forage on pasture, and the eggs have bright orange yolks and truly are so flavorful they are worth writing home about. Their dairy products are raw and unprocessed, and easily digestible. If you have an opportunity to purchase this type of eggs or dairy, please do for the sheer pleasure of tasting such delicious food. Most of the aged cheeses, such as Cheddar, Gruyère, and blue, used in this book can be readily found in raw milk varieties in gourmet markets. Otherwise, get the best quality that you can, preferably organic. I am not an advocate of heavily processed dairy products and those labeled "low fat." Real whole dairy, unprocessed or traditionally cultured, is by far the tastiest and healthiest choice.

Use good-quality stable fats and oils that can be heated without becoming rancid or oxidized. These include extra virgin olive oil, organic butter, unrefined sesame oil, toasted sesame oil, and coconut oil. I use pumpkinseed oil and walnut oil for salads and condiments. Coconut oil, long vilified, is just now getting praise for being the healthy traditional oil that it has always been. For cooking, I use a variety that is filtered so as not to have the distinctive flavor of coconut in all my dishes. Food sautéed in coconut oil is noticeably less greasy and light on the body.

I favor good-quality sea salt, with a high mineral content; my favorite is Celtic sea salt, with more than eighty minerals intact. Salt draws the constituent flavors together in a dish and leaves a rounded feeling on the tongue. The right amount of salt—not too little, but not too much to make your dish salty—is what makes the flavors in a dish soar.

I prefer natural sugars too. My favorite sugar is maple sugar, a pricey variety when you buy it in a store, but economical if you buy it directly from the producers. (See Resources, page 251.) I use Sucanat (unrefined cane sugar) too, and evaporated cane sugar when I need a sweetener with a less pronounced flavor. Although this variety is subjected to a substantial amount of processing, it is not as refined as white sugar. Furthermore, it's organic, an important detail when using such a highly concentrated substance. I favor maple or rice syrup when syrups are the best choice of sweetener.

PANTRY

These items are all used in more than one holiday menu.

On the Shelves

NUTS AND DRIED FRUIT: pistachios, blanched almonds, sesame seeds, pine nuts, dried currants, dried cherries, walnuts, prunes, pumpkinseeds, dried unsweetened coconut, raisins, hazelnuts, almonds, pecans

OILS AND VINEGARS: extra virgin olive oil, coconut oil, red wine vinegar, balsamic vinegar, brown rice vinegar, dry sherry, mirin, shoyu (natural soy sauce)

BEANS AND GRAINS: red lentils, quinoa, pinto beans, corn grits, wild rice

FLOURS: cornmeal, unbleached white flour, whole wheat pastry flour

SUGARS: rice syrup, raw honey, maple sugar, Florida crystals, maple syrup, Sucanat

CANS AND PACKAGES: 15-ounce cans diced tomatoes, canned plum tomatoes, dried porcini mushrooms, cans of chickpeas, unsweetened coconut milk

SPICES: sea salt, cloves, cinnamon, dried oregano, saffron, cayenne, fenugreek, cumin seeds, ground cumin, coriander seeds, ground coriander, hot red pepper flakes, paprika, saffron, caraway seed, smoked paprika, thyme, chili powder, ground ginger, allspice, fennel, nutmeg, whole black peppercorns, dried oregano, bay leaf, fresh nutmeg, whole dried chipotle chile

BAKING: baking powder, baking soda, vanilla extract, almond extract, unsweetened chocolate, bittersweet chocolate, semisweet chocolate, cocoa powder, semisweet chocolate chips, soy milk

IN THE REFRIGERATOR: Dijon mustard, tube tomato paste, white wine, roasted red peppers, kalamata olives, green olives, pumpkinseed oil, unsalted butter, milk, apple cider, sauerkraut, capers, vanilla beans, beer, anchovies, light miso, prepared horseradish

These pantry items are used for a specific holiday:

RAMADAN: sliced almonds, Indian red chiles or chiles de arbol, semolina flour, orange blossom water

THANKSGIVING: guajillo chile, ancho chiles, chipotle chile in adobo sauce, dried cranberries, crystallized ginger, gingersnaps

CHRISTMAS EVE: spelt berries, poppy seeds, barley, large lima beans, Madeira, dried apricots

CHRISTMAS DAY: great Northern beans, 28-ounce cans crushed tomatoes, hazelnuts, lasagna noodles

KWANZAA: New Mexican chiles, Indian red chiles, turmeric, cardamom pods, ground cardamom, mustard seeds, brandy, teff flour

NEW YEAR'S EVE: cocoa nibs, grape leaves, cannellini beans

NEW YEAR'S DAY: black-eyed peas, almond butter

CHINESE NEW YEAR: peanut butter, toasted sesame oil, unrefined sesame oil, goji berries, Szechuan peppercorns, five-spice powder, fermented black beans, dried shiitake mushrooms, long noodles

VALENTINE'S DAY: sherry vinegar, port, sun-dried tomatoes, French lentils, oat flour

ST. PATRICK'S DAY: rolled oats, marjoram

PASSOVER: matzo meal, walnut oil, dates

EASTER: rose water, instant tapioca

CINCO DE MAYO: pasilla chiles, chiles de arbol

FOURTH OF JULY: tequila, sun-dried tomatoes

Equipment

There are a few pieces of equipment I call for that are of special importance, but none are so unusual that you won't use them time and time again. It's important to have a large roasting pan, along with a roasting rack, for the Thanksgiving turkey and the chicken for Chinese New Year. A bulb baster and

defatting cup are handy for the turkey. You'll need a couple of 8 by 8-inch
(1-quart) and 8 by 11-inch (2-quart) baking dishes (I recommend Pyrex) for
a variety of dishes in the book. Also useful are a springform cake pan, 9-inch
tart pan, 9 by 5-inch loaf pan, and 9-inch pie plates. Ceramic half-cup ramekins are great for the crème caramel from Cinco de Mayo and the Semifreddo Affogato from New Year's Eve. I like to have available a stack of
disposable aluminum ramekins for the Valentine's Day Belgian Brownies.
(See Resources, page 251.) A blender and food processor are two essential
pieces of equipment. A spice grinder (use an inexpensive coffee mill) is convenient for spices, and a stand mixer or handheld mixer is necessary to whip
up cookie dough or aerate eggs. I find a myriad of uses for my cast-iron skillet, including toasting nuts, seeds, and spices, and a grill or grill pan is important for the Fourth of July menu.

Basic Techniques

ROASTING GARLIC: Preheat the oven to 350°F. Peel off the papery outer layers
of the garlic head and cut off the top fifth. Lay the head on a piece of aluminum foil large enough to enfold the garlic. Drizzle with a teaspoon of
extra virgin olive oil and a sprinkling of salt. Wrap in foil and roast for
about 40 minutes, until the garlic is tender and golden brown. Remove
from the oven and let cool a few minutes before squeezing the garlic paste
out of the cloves.

TO PEEL AND SEED TOMATOES: Bring a pot of water to a boil. Cut out the core of
the tomato with the tip of a paring knife. Drop the tomatoes in boiling
water for 15 to 30 seconds, depending on the ripeness. Remove the tomatoes with a slotted spoon and let cool a minute. The skins should peel
right off. To seed, cut the tomatoes in half through the equator and
squeeze out the seeds.

TOASTING SPICES: Dry-toast whole spices in a heavy-bottomed skillet (a cast-
iron skillet is ideal) over medium heat, stirring frequently, until fragrant,
2 to 3 minutes. Transfer to a spice grinder or mortar and pestle and grind
into powder.

CITRUS SUPREMES: Cut a disk off the top and bottom of each citrus. Next, cut
downward, following the contours of the fruit, to slice the peel off the cit-

rus, exposing the flesh. Holding the fruit over a bowl to collect the juices, use a paring knife to separate the segments from the inner membranes by slicing down to the core on either side of each segment.

SOAKING BEANS OR GRAINS: You can soak your beans overnight with cold water to cover, or hot-soak them by placing them in a pot, covering with cold water, and bringing them to a boil. Turn off the heat and let them sit, covered, for 1 hour to absorb the water. Either way, drain the beans and start with fresh cold water to cook.

TO THICKEN YOGURT: Place 2 cups yogurt (preferably whole milk) in a cheesecloth-lined strainer over a bowl. Place the yogurt in the refrigerator and let it drain for at least 2 hours and up to overnight. Two cups of yogurt will yield 1 cup of thickened yogurt.

CLEANING OUT YOUR SPICE GRINDER: To get rid of the potent odor of whatever spice you may have ground, place a handful of white rice or a piece of bread in the grinder, grind it, and then discard.

BREAD CUBES AND BREAD CRUMBS: Remove the crusts from day-old or stale bread and slice into cubes. Process the cubes in the food processor until crumbs. If the bread is too fresh and spongy, slice it and put it in a 200°F oven for a few minutes to dry a bit before processing. Make a large batch and freeze any leftover bread crumbs in a resealable bag. Bread crumbs defrost almost immediately. Freeze some of the cubes for homemade croutons, and freeze some of the whole slices for when you need a bread thickener (Ribollita Soup, Tomatillo-Pumpkin Mole).

TOASTING NUTS AND SEEDS: Spread nuts or seeds on a baking sheet and toast in a preheated 350°F oven for 8 to 10 minutes, until lightly golden and fragrant. Pine nuts take only about 6 minutes. Alternatively, dry-toast the nuts or seeds in a heavy-bottomed skillet, stirring frequently, until brown spots begin to appear, about 3 minutes.

WALNUTS have a loose skin that often dislodges when they are chopped. After toasting, rub the walnuts against a strainer for a minute or two (over the sink or a wastebasket) to loosen the skins. Remove the walnuts from the strainer, leaving the skins behind.

TO REMOVE SKINS FROM HAZELNUTS: Toast the hazelnuts in the oven for 8 to 10 minutes, until the papery skins start to loosen. Wrap the hazelnuts while still warm in a kitchen towel and rub them against one another to loosen the skins. Remove the cleaned hazelnuts to a bowl. Repeat several times with the remaining nuts until most of the skins are removed.

ROASTED BELL PEPPERS: Place a pepper directly on the grate over a gas burner. Turn the heat to high and leave to cook until the side is blistered and charred. Use tongs to turn the pepper and cook each side until the whole surface is blackened. This should take only a few minutes. Place the peppers in a plastic or paper bag or under an inverted bowl for about 15 minutes to steam the skin loose. When the pepper is cool enough to handle, remove the charred skin, using a paring knife if necessary. Don't run the pepper under water to remove the skin, as that washes away a lot of flavor. Discard the seeds and stem and slice the peppers into thin slices.

Alternatively, halve the peppers and place them, cut side down, on an oiled or parchment-covered baking sheet. Place in a 450°F oven or under a broiler. Roast or broil until evenly charred. Remove from the oven or broiler, cover immediately, and proceed with the directions for removing the skin.

CULINARY ASSUMPTIONS

- All olive oil is extra virgin olive oil
- All eggs are large
- All butter is unsalted
- All white flour is unbleached all-purpose white flour
- All milk is whole
- Yogurt is plain, full fat
- Cheese is full fat
- All coconut oil is expeller pressed filtered with no coconut flavor
- All black pepper is freshly ground
- 1 onion is 6 ounces, which makes 1 cup chopped
- 1 garlic clove makes 1 teaspoon minced
- 8 by 8-inch baking dish is 1 quart
- 8 by 11-inch baking dish is 2 quarts

Ramadan
The Feast of Eid al Fitr

- Roasted Red Pepper Pesto with Almonds and Sesame Seeds 16

- Turkish Red Lentil Soup 17

- Green Leaf Salad with Crispy Shallots and Pomegranate Molasses Dressing 18

- Chicken Breasts Stuffed with Onions, Cinnamon, Almonds, and Cherries 20

- Chickpea Charmoula Strudel 21

- Quinoa-Carrot Pilaf with Saffron, Mint, and Spiced Carrots 24

- Harissa Spinach 25

- Semolina Walnut Cake with Macerated Oranges 26

RAMADAN IS THE MOST important holiday in Islam, falling on the entire ninth month of the Muslim lunar calendar, sometime between October and February on the Western calendar. Ramadan commemorates the month that Muslims believe their holy book, the Koran, was divinely revealed to the prophet Mohammed.

The entire month is spent fasting every day from sunup to sundown and engaging in other ascetic practices. During this time of worship and contemplation, Muslims start afresh, give their life new direction, and concentrate more on faith and less on the mundane. It is a time for forgiveness, renewal of family ties, and focusing on inner peace. The aim of such intensive fasting is to learn self-restraint, a quality that helps temper aggressive tendencies and control desires. Besides fasting, one must renounce one's bad habits. The prophet Mohammed is reputed to have said that those who cling to their evil ways get only thirst and hunger from fasting. At the end of each day, the fast is broken with prayer and a meal called the *iftar* (usually dates are the first food with which one breaks the fast). Then it is customary to go out visiting family and friends. The fast resumes the next morning.

Ramadan ends with the feast of Eid al Fitr, the Festival of Breaking the Fast, a time of great jubilation after having ended a difficult month. The three-day festival takes place after the new moon of the tenth month. People don their best garments, go to special prayers at the mosque, decorate their homes, visit family and friends, give children gifts and money, and aid the less fortunate. It's a joyful holiday, a time for being thankful for the help and strength that helped one get through the previous month of self-control, a day of forgetting old grudges and ill feelings toward others.

Though the dishes served at the feast may vary, since the Muslim community extends throughout many different countries, the celebration involves eating lavishly and abundantly. The Middle Eastern menu here draws predominantly on my favorite flavors from Morocco and Turkey. The meal begins with a roasted red pepper and sesame seed dip and a Turkish red lentil soup. The vegetarian main course is a savory strudel of chickpeas seasoned with the Moroccan herb and spice mix known as charmoula. An alternative main course is chicken breasts stuffed with caramelized onions, dried fruit, and almonds. Pomegranate molasses vinaigrette dresses the salad, and spicy harissa lends excitement to a dish of spinach. The feast finishes with a semolina walnut cake laced with orange blossom water.

Cook's Notes

Up to 2 weeks in advance:

Make the chickpea strudel and freeze.

Up to 2 days in advance:

Make the red pepper pesto.
Make the soup (you can make it up to two weeks ahead and freeze).

Day before:

Bake the cake.
Make the salad dressing.
Make the macerated oranges for the cake.
Make the caramelized onion filling for the chicken.
Seed the pomegranate for the garnish.
Wash and dry the spinach for the harissa greens. Store in a ziplock bag with paper towels.

Day of:

Stuff and cook the chicken.
Roast the carrots and cook the quinoa.
Cook the harissa greens.
Wash the salad greens.
Toast the pita triangles.

Last minute:

Bake the strudel.
Toss the salad.

Roasted Red Pepper Pesto with Almonds and Sesame Seeds

SESAME SEEDS give this robust dip an exciting Middle Eastern flair. Serve with toasted pita wedges as your guests arrive.

The dip will keep, refrigerated, for a week.

MAKES 1 HEAPING CUP

$1/2$ cup whole almonds
$1/4$ cup sesame seeds
1 red bell pepper, roasted, or $1/2$ cup jarred roasted red pepper
5 tablespoons extra virgin olive oil
1 tablespoon red wine vinegar
1 tablespoon fresh lemon juice
Salt and freshly ground black pepper
$1/4$ teaspoon cayenne pepper
2 tablespoons chopped fresh parsley, for garnish

In a medium skillet over medium heat, dry-toast the almonds until lightly browned, about 3 minutes. Remove from the heat and set aside. Dry-toast the sesame seeds until lightly golden, about 1 minute. Set aside.

Place the pepper in a food processor along with the almonds, oil, vinegar, lemon juice, $1/2$ teaspoon salt, a generous sprinkling of black pepper, and the cayenne. Process until smooth.

Add the sesame seeds and pulse to combine. Transfer to a bowl and serve sprinkled with parsley.

Turkish Red Lentil Soup

THIS SMOOTH fragrant soup will be delicious made with water. Cooking it with roasted vegetable stock, however, makes it truly deep and flavorful.

For the freshest taste start with whole cumin, coriander, and fenugreek seeds and grind them in a spice grinder. Fenugreek, a slightly bitter spice used in a lot of Indian and Middle Eastern cooking, joins harmoniously with the other flavors, so don't skip it. If you can't find it locally, it can be ordered from Penzey's, Worldspice, and Kalustyan's (see Resources, page 251).

SERVES 5

2 tablespoons extra virgin olive oil
2 medium onions, cut into small dice (2 cups)
1 medium carrot, peeled and cut into small dice (½ cup)
4 garlic cloves, minced
1½ teaspoons ground cumin seed
1½ teaspoons ground coriander seed
1 teaspoon ground fenugreek
¼ teaspoon red pepper flakes
One 15-ounce can diced tomatoes, preferably fire-roasted
5 cups water, All-Purpose Vegetable Stock (page 6), or Roasted Root Vegetable Stock
    (page 4)
¾ cup red lentils
Salt and freshly ground black pepper

Garnish
½ cup chopped fresh dill
1 cup plain yogurt or sour cream

Warm the olive oil in a medium pot or saucepan over medium heat. Add the onions and sauté for 10 minutes, until softened and lightly browned. Add the carrot, garlic, cumin, coriander, fenugreek, and red pepper flakes and sauté for 1 minute.

Stir in the tomatoes and scrape up any brown bits in the pan. Simmer for 5 minutes, until the

(continued)

tomato liquid reduces by half. Add the water or stock and lentils, cover, and bring the liquid to a boil. Lower the heat, add 1 1/4 teaspoons salt, and simmer, partially covered, until the lentils are softened, about 20 to 25 minutes. Transfer the soup to a blender and purée until smooth. Return the soup to the pot and add a sprinkling of black pepper. Taste and adjust the salt if necessary.

MAKE THE GARNISH: Stir 1/4 cup of the dill into the yogurt.

Serve the soup hot, with a dollop of the dill yogurt. Sprinkle with the remaining dill.

Green Leaf Salad with Crispy Shallots and Pomegranate Molasses Dressing

THIS IS a delightful salad of unusual flavors and textures. Pomegranate molasses is the sweet-and-sour reduced syrup from pomegranates enjoyed in many Middle Eastern countries. It is readily available in Middle Eastern stores and gourmet markets.

The shallots flavor the olive oil deliciously as they caramelize, leaving crispy shallots for the salad and an infused oil for the dressing. You will have just enough juice from cutting up the oranges to make the 2 tablespoons that you need.

SERVES 6

1/2 cup extra virgin olive oil
1/2 cup shallots, cut into thin rings
2 navel oranges
1/2 teaspoon Dijon mustard
2 tablespoons pomegranate molasses
2 tablespoons fresh orange juice
Salt and freshly ground black pepper
8 cups green leaf lettuce (1/2 pound), torn into pieces
1/2 cup pomegranate seeds

Have ready a strainer set over a small bowl.

Warm the oil with the shallots in a small skillet over medium-low heat. Simmer just until the shallots are golden, about 10 minutes. Keep a close eye on the shallots as they start to turn golden brown, then stir frequently to let them color evenly. Do not let them burn. Remove from the heat and strain the oil immediately (to keep the shallots from cooking further), reserving the oil and the shallots separately.

Cut the peel and any white pith from the oranges with a sharp knife, then cut the sections free from the membranes, letting them drop into a medium bowl. You will have enough juice from the oranges to get the 2 tablespoons you need for the dressing.

In a small bowl, whisk together the mustard, pomegranate molasses, and orange juice with a sprinkling of salt and black pepper. Whisk in the shallot oil. You should have 1/2 cup of dressing.

Mix the lettuce in a salad bowl with the orange slices, reserved shallots, and pomegranate seeds. Sprinkle the greens with salt and pepper. Toss with the dressing, divide among plates, and serve immediately.

Chicken Breasts Stuffed with Onions, Cinnamon, Almonds, and Cherries

*T*HIS IS a sensational party dish that always gets raves from guests. Savory foods cooked with dried fruits are common in Morocco. Here, onions, cherries, and sliced almonds are cooked together and stuffed into chicken breasts, which are breaded, sautéed, and finished in the oven, then sliced into medallions to serve. The stuffing keeps the breast meat exceptionally moist, so it's a wonderful dish to make a day in advance.

SERVES 6 TO 8

¼ cup extra virgin olive oil
3 cups thinly sliced onions
¼ cup sliced almonds, toasted
½ cup dried cherries or raisins, plumped in warm water and drained
2 tablespoons maple or evaporated cane sugar
2 teaspoons ground cinnamon
Salt and freshly ground black pepper
4 boneless chicken breasts
¾ cup unbleached white flour
2 eggs
2 cups bread crumbs, preferably fresh from a sourdough or country loaf
Extra virgin olive oil or coconut oil, for sautéing

Warm the oil in a medium skillet. Add the onions and sauté over medium heat until tender, about 6 minutes. Stir in the almonds, cherries, sugar, cinnamon, ½ teaspoon salt, and a sprinkling of black pepper. Cook, stirring frequently, until the onions are deeply golden, about 15 minutes.

Trim, rinse, and pat the breasts dry. Remove the tenderloin (the small hanging piece) and set aside.

Using a sharp boning or utility knife, cut into the breast about ½ inch from one end. Create a pocket, slicing to within about ¼ inch of the other side.

Stuff each breast with about ½ cup of the filling, distributing it evenly throughout the pocket and to the ends. Press on the top of each breast to close the pocket.

Line up 3 wide shallow dishes or bowls. Fill the first with the flour. Lightly beat the eggs in the second dish. Toss the bread crumbs in the third dish with 1/2 teaspoon salt and 1/2 teaspoon pepper.

Season the breasts generously on both sides with salt and pepper. Dredge one breast well in the flour, shaking off any excess. Dip it into the eggs, turning to coat evenly, and then dredge it in the bread crumbs, pressing to make the crumbs adhere evenly. Gently shake off any excess. Set the breast on a plate and repeat with the remaining breasts.

Refrigerate the breaded chicken for at least 5 minutes and up to 3 hours to let the coating set. Bread the tenderloins also. Discard any leftover flour, egg, or bread crumbs.

Heat the oven to 350°F.

Film a large nonstick skillet with oil and heat over medium-high heat. When the oil is very hot (a hand held 1 inch over the pan should feel hot), carefully add 2 breasts to the pan (it should sizzle) and cook until golden brown, about 3 minutes per side. If the oil gets too hot, reduce the heat to medium. Transfer the breasts to a baking tray. Repeat with the other 2 breasts.

Cook the tenderloins until golden brown and firm to the touch, about 3 minutes per side. Serve them along with the medallions or save them for a tasty snack.

Place the tray in the oven and bake until the chicken feels firm to the touch (it will register 165°F on an instant-read thermometer), about 15 minutes. Remove from the oven and slice into 1-inch-thick medallions. Serve hot.

You can place the cut medallions in a baking dish, cover, and refrigerate. They stay moist, even when reheated.

chickpea charmoula strudel

CHARMOULA IS a Moroccan spice and herb mixture made from olive oil, lemon juice, paprika, cumin, garlic, parsley, and cilantro. Though it is traditionally used to season fish, here it is cooked with chickpeas, green olives, and tomatoes and baked into a vegetarian phyllo strudel, which looks beautiful when sliced and plated. This is a great dish to make in advance, since it can be baked directly from the freezer at a moment's notice (see page 23).

(continued)

MAKES 2 STRUDELS (SERVES 6)

2 tablespoons extra virgin olive oil, plus more for the phyllo

2 cups finely diced onion

1 garlic clove, minced

4 plum tomatoes, peeled and seeded, or one 14-ounce can plum tomatoes, drained and
    roughly chopped

2 teaspoons paprika

2 teaspoons ground cumin

15 green olives, pitted and roughly chopped (¼ cup)

3 tablespoons fresh lemon juice

One 15-ounce can chickpeas, drained and rinsed, or 1½ cups cooked chickpeas

¾ teaspoon salt

2 tablespoons chopped fresh cilantro

¼ cup chopped fresh parsley

⅛ teaspoon cayenne pepper

¾ pound phyllo dough (12 sheets)

Warm 2 tablespoons of the oil in a large skillet. Add the onion and garlic and cook over medium-low heat, stirring occasionally, being careful not to let the garlic burn, for about 10 minutes, until the onions are tender and the garlic is golden brown. Stir in the tomatoes, paprika, cumin, olives, and lemon juice and cook, uncovered, for 1 minute. Stir in the chickpeas and salt. Cover and cook for 5 minutes to marry the flavors. Remove from the heat, mash half the chickpeas, then stir in the cilantro, parsley, and cayenne until well combined. Transfer to a bowl to cool.

Preheat the oven to 425°F. Line a baking sheet with parchment.

Remove 12 sheets from the package of phyllo. Rewrap the remaining sheets and refrigerate for another use. Cover the sheets with a kitchen towel. Place a damp towel on top of the dry one to keep the moisture in. Have ready a pastry brush and a ramekin with olive oil.

Remove a piece of phyllo from the stack, set it on a clean surface or piece of parchment, and brush with a light layer of oil, making sure to coat all the edges. Pull off another sheet, place it on top of the first, and brush that one with oil as well. Continue layering and brushing with oil until you have 6 stacked, oiled sheets. Leave the remaining 6 unused sheets beneath the towel.

Spread half of the chickpea mixture in an even, rounded, 2-inch-wide strip at one of the long ends of the phyllo stack, leaving a 1½-inch border on the sides and bottom. Fold the border over to partially cover the filling and brush the folded edge with oil. Starting from the folded edge, roll the phyllo into a tight log and brush with oil on all sides. At this point you can wrap and freeze the strudels until you are ready to bake them. Repeat the entire process with the remaining phyllo sheets and the second half of the filling.

Place the strudels on the prepared baking sheet. Score the strudels with even-angled cuts, making sure not to cut into the filling, to divide each log into 6 to 12 pieces, depending on the size you want. Bake the strudels until golden brown, 15 to 20 minutes. Cut each strudel at the scored sections, and serve hot.

Using Phyllo

Keep the phyllo covered at all times. Open the package of phyllo, lay the unrolled sheets on a sheet of parchment or wax paper, and cover them with a kitchen towel. Place a damp towel on top of the dry ones to keep the moisture in. After you pull out a sheet, cover the stack right away. Phyllo dries out rapidly.

The dough defrosts quickly at room temperature, but it defrosts best in the refrigerator. Once defrosted, it keeps about a week refrigerated. You can roll up and even refreeze phyllo you have not used if it has not been exposed to air.

Phyllo is forgiving. Even if it tears or crinkles, chances are by the time you fold it or layer it, you won't even notice.

Be sure to brush oil or melted butter between all the layers. The fat is what pushes the layer of dough up, making the phyllo flaky. It doesn't matter what kind of fat you use as long as you use something. Brush a thin film between all the layers of phyllo. If you fold it, remember to brush another layer. Always spread a layer on the completed piece or the phyllo will be too dry. Use a pastry brush to brush the fat and don't douse the dough—a thin layer is best.

All filled phyllo can be frozen before baking. To freeze, spread on a baking sheet. When it is frozen solid, after a couple of hours, you can stack the strudels however you like. Spread them on a baking sheet without defrosting when you are ready to bake them. You need only an additional 5 minutes or so of baking time if they have been frozen. Phyllo that is not filled, like cups or pastries that have a dry filling, can be baked up to a week in advance and kept covered in a container at room temperature.

Quinoa-Carrot Pilaf with Saffron, Mint, and Spiced Carrots

DELICATE QUINOA is teamed with aromatic spices as a tasty and balancing counterpoint to the more piquant greens. Couscous would be the traditional accompaniment for the dish, but I've opted for quinoa because of its superior nutritional value.

SERVES 6

1¼ cups quinoa
2½ cups water
Pinch of saffron
½ teaspoon salt, plus additional for seasoning
¾ pound carrots, cut into ¾-inch dice (2 cups)
1 teaspoon ground cumin
¼ teaspoon ground cinnamon
1 tablespoon extra virgin olive oil
2 tablespoons chopped fresh mint
1 tablespoon fresh lemon juice
Freshly ground black pepper

Preheat the oven to 375°F.

Rinse the quinoa in a strainer. Dry-toast it in a medium pot over medium-high heat, stirring constantly, until the grains smell fragrant and are almost dry. Stir in the water, saffron, and ¼ teaspoon salt, scraping up any grains that have stuck to the bottom. Cover, bring to a boil, then lower the heat to a simmer. Cook, covered, until the grains have swelled and the water is absorbed, about 15 minutes. Do not disturb the steam vents that will form while the quinoa is cooking.

Meanwhile, mix the carrots in a small bowl with the cumin, cinnamon, oil, and the remaining ¼ teaspoon salt. Spread them on a parchment-covered baking sheet and roast until tender, about 20 minutes.

Transfer the carrots to the pot with the quinoa, and stir in the mint and lemon juice. Sprinkle with black pepper. Add additional salt to taste. Serve hot.

Harissa Spinach

*H*ARISSA IS a fiery Moroccan spice mixture of chile peppers, cumin, coriander, and caraway that enlivens any dish. The *picante* greens are complemented perfectly by the cool, minty flavor of the quinoa-carrot dish.

If you don't have a small coffee grinder that you can use as a spice mill, lightly dry-toast the seeds in a heavy-bottomed skillet and crush them in a mortar and pestle or with a rolling pin.

SERVES 6 GENEROUSLY

12 dried small hot red chile peppers, such as Indian chiles, chiles de arbol, or whole
    cayenne (about 2 tablespoons)
1 teaspoon caraway seed
1 teaspoon cumin seed
1 teaspoon coriander seed
1 garlic clove, minced
1 jalapeño pepper, stemmed, seeded, and minced
2 tablespoons extra virgin olive oil
2 pounds spinach, stems removed, washed, and roughly cut into small pieces
    (approximately 10 cups)
½ teaspoon salt

Remove the seeds and stems from the chiles and discard. Place the chiles in a small pot covered with water. Bring to a boil, turn off the heat, and let the chiles sit in the hot water until softened, about 10 minutes.

Meanwhile, grind the spices together in a spice mill.

Chop the softened chiles into small pieces. You should have 1 tablespoon. Transfer them to a small bowl and add the garlic, jalapeño, and spices.

Warm the oil and chile-spice mixture together in a large skillet over medium heat. Cook until the garlic begins to turn straw colored, about 3 minutes, being careful not to burn. Stir in the spinach, a large handful at a time. Cook until the spinach is wilted, tossing it with tongs, continuing to add more until all of the greens are in the pan. Stir in the salt. Cover and cook for 5 minutes, until the spinach is completely wilted and tender. Uncover and raise the heat. Cook, uncovered, stirring constantly, for about 5 minutes, until most of the liquid is evaporated. Serve hot.

Semolina Walnut Cake with Macerated Oranges

*T*HE HEADY essence of orange blossoms is everywhere in Marrakech, from fountains to desserts. Macerated oranges, scented with orange blossom water, are draped over the nutty-textured cake, giving it a puddinglike consistency and festive appearance.

MAKES ONE 9-INCH CAKE

SERVES 8 TO 10

1 ½ cups walnuts, toasted and ground (see Note)

¼ cup unbleached white or whole wheat pastry flour

¾ cup semolina flour

1 cup sugar, preferably maple or evaporated cane sugar (Florida crystals)

2 teaspoons baking powder

¾ teaspoon salt

4 eggs

½ cup water

1 teaspoon vanilla extract

Grated zest of 1 orange

2 teaspoons orange blossom water

6 tablespoons extra virgin olive oil

Macerated Oranges

4 oranges

½ teaspoon ground cinnamon

½ teaspoon orange blossom water

1 tablespoon honey

MAKE THE CAKE: Preheat the oven to 325°F. Oil a 9-inch cake or springform pan and line the bottom with parchment paper.

Whisk the walnuts, flour, semolina, sugar, baking powder, and salt together in a medium bowl.

In another medium bowl, whisk together the eggs, water, vanilla, orange zest, and orange blossom water until thoroughly combined. Pour the wet mixture into the dry ingredients, mixing just until the dry ingredients are moistened. Stir in the olive oil and mix until thoroughly combined.

Pour the batter into the prepared baking pan and place in the middle rack in the oven. Bake 35 minutes, or until the cake is golden and lightly cracked and a toothpick inserted in the middle comes out dry. Remove the cake from the oven and let cool in the pan for 10 minutes, then release the cake, pull off the parchment paper, and let the cake continue to cool while you make the topping.

MAKE THE TOPPING: Cut a disk off the top and bottom of each orange. Cut away the peel and any white pith from the orange with a sharp knife. Slice the orange into ¼-inch rounds.

Place the rounds in a medium bowl along with the cinnamon, orange blossom water, and honey. Let sit for 20 minutes to macerate.

Serve the cake with the oranges and their juice draped over the cake.

Note: To toast walnuts, preheat the oven to 350°F. Spread the nuts on a baking sheet and toast 7 to 9 minutes, until fragrant. Let the nuts cool on a plate before grinding them into a coarse meal in a food processor or blender.

Thanksgiving

ERHAPS THE MOST WIDELY celebrated American holiday, Thanksgiving is about gathering with family and friends in the spirit of gratitude. Each year, people travel great distances to sit down to dinner with their loved ones on the last Thursday of November.

The practice of expressing gratitude for the bounty of the harvest extends far back in human history. Although the Pilgrims never had an annual Thanksgiving, the large feast they had in 1621 to celebrate their first harvest in Plymouth is the model for the Thanksgiving celebration in the United States. The outdoor feast included ninety Native Americans, lasted three days, and included enough wildfowl and other foods to supply the whole village for a week. Although not typical of what later happened between Native Americans and the first Europeans, this mythologized moment in our nation's history evokes the spirit of the modern-day holiday.

Thanksgiving celebrations were observed irregularly afterward. In 1789, George Washington proclaimed that November 26 be a day of thanksgiving and prayer. Again in 1863, Abraham Lincoln declared Thanksgiving a national holiday and issued a proclamation: "The year that is drawing towards its close, has been filled with the blessing of fruitful fields and healthful skies." Since then, the holiday has been observed annually, and every president has issued a Thanksgiving proclamation. In 1939, under President Roosevelt, the date was changed to the fourth Thursday in November.

More than any other holiday in America, Thanksgiving is about the food. Abraham Lincoln and Ulysses S. Grant made turkey a tradition when they ordered it served to all the troops on the holiday. Cranberries and sweet potatoes are even more recent additions to the traditional menu, not appearing until the advent of canned foods in the 1870s.

The harvest feast presented here, utilizing the best of the season's produce, is inspired by Southwestern and Native American flavors. The turkey is dry-brined with a smoky rub and served with a pumpkinseed mole gravy. The vegetarian main course is a Native American three sisters stew consisting of corn, beans, and squash baked between layers of a corn grits polenta crust. All the trimmings, sides, and desserts are included to please a large array of palates, from the traditionalist to the most adventuresome. The requisite sweet potatoes are spiced with chipotle chile and baked with coconut milk, and the cranberry relish is brightened with persimmons and ginger. Brussels sprouts are caramelized, then braised in beer, mustard, and honey; autumn greens, flavored with crushed garlic, are studded with pearl onions. The wild rice and bread cube dressing is flavored with a porcini mushroom broth and flecked with pine nuts. While the butternut semifreddo and apple-pear-cranberry pie desserts are included in this menu, the Sweet Potato Pie from the New Year's Day menu is a great choice too.

Cook's Notes

Up to 2 weeks in advance:

Assemble the apple pie and freeze.
Make the butternut semifreddo and freeze.
Make the chicken or roasted vegetable stock and freeze.

Up to 3 days in advance:

Make the cranberry-persimmon sauce.
Make the base for the mole gravy.
Put together the rub for the turkey.

Up to 2 days in advance:

Make the filling for the Three Sisters Polenta Casserole.
Make the black bean dip.

Day before:

Cook the polenta and assemble and bake the three sisters casserole.
Make the sweet potato gratin.

Make the wild rice dressing.

Rub the spice rub on the turkey and refrigerate, uncovered.

Prepare the crudités for the dip.

Day of:

Remove the turkey from the refrigerator and let sit for 1 hour.

Bake the apple-pear-cranberry pie while the turkey sits.

Cook the turkey. While the turkey is cooking, make the brussels sprouts and the braised autumn greens.

While the turkey is resting, reheat the wild rice dressing, the sweet potato gratin, and the three sisters casserole. Finish the mole gravy.

An hour before dessert, transfer the butternut semifreddo to the refrigerator.

Southwestern Black Bean Dip

*E*NJOY THIS smooth dip with an assortment of crudités or tortilla chips while your guests are gathering.

MAKES 3 ½ CUPS

1 ½ cups black beans, soaked overnight or hot-soaked (see page 11)

4 cups water

6 garlic cloves, peeled and left whole

1 cup chopped onion

1 dried guajillo chile, stemmed and seeded

1 ½ teaspoons salt

¼ cup extra virgin olive oil

1 teaspoon cumin, toasted and ground (see page 10)

½ cup thinly sliced scallions, white and green parts

½ cup chopped cilantro

2 serrano chiles, stemmed and seeded

2 tablespoons fresh lime juice

Drain the beans and place them in a medium saucepan along with the water, garlic, onion, chile, and 1 teaspoon of the salt. Bring to a boil, lower the heat, and cook, partially covered, about 1 hour, until the beans are tender. Or use a pressure cooker with 3 cups water and the garlic, onion, chile, and 1 teaspoon salt. Bring to a boil, lock in the lid, and cook under high pressure 10 minutes. Let the pressure return to normal.

Drain the beans, reserving the cooking liquid. Remove and discard the dried chile. Transfer the beans to a food processor and add the oil, cumin, and the remaining ½ teaspoon salt. Process until smooth, adding a little bean cooking liquid if necessary for a creamy texture. Add the scallions, cilantro, serrano chiles, and lime juice and process until well combined. Serve at room temperature.

Three Sisters Polenta Casserole with Pumpkinseed Pesto

NATIVE AMERICANS have traditionally grown corn, beans, and squash as companion crops for hundreds of years. They bring out the best in one another in this satisfying vegetarian main course as well. A harvest stew, nestled between layers of polenta, is topped with pumpkinseed pesto to round out the flavors. The casserole slices beautifully, and can be made ahead and refrigerated until you are ready to bake it and serve it to your guests.

ONE 8 X 11-INCH CASSEROLE (SERVES 8 TO 12)

¾ cup pinto or appaloosa beans, soaked overnight or hot-soaked (see page 11)

4 cups water

1 teaspoon salt, plus extra for seasoning

2 tablespoons extra virgin olive oil

2 cups onion, diced small

2 bell peppers, preferably 1 yellow and 1 red, cut into 1-inch dice

2 garlic cloves, minced

1 teaspoon ground coriander

1 teaspoon ground cumin

½ teaspoon smoked paprika

1 jalapeño pepper, stemmed, seeded, and minced

2 cups squash (from 1 pound kabocha or butternut squash), cut into ¾-inch dice

One 14-ounce can diced tomatoes

1 cup fresh or frozen corn kernels

Polenta

4½ cups water

1½ cups corn grits

¾ teaspoon salt

1 tablespoon chili powder, preferably New Mexican

1 tablespoon butter (optional)

1 tablespoon extra virgin olive oil, for baking

Pumpkinseed Pesto (recipe follows)

Place the beans in a small pot with the water and ½ teaspoon of the salt. Cover and bring to a boil. Lower the heat and simmer, partially covered, until softened, about 45 minutes to 1 hour. Drain, reserving ½ cup of the cooking liquid. (Alternatively, pressure-cook the beans at high pressure for 10 minutes.)

Warm the olive oil in a medium saucepan. Add the onions and cook over medium heat until softened, about 7 minutes. Add the bell peppers and cook an additional 5 minutes.

Stir in the garlic, spices, jalapeño, squash, and tomatoes. Cook, uncovered, stirring from time to time, for 5 minutes. Add the reserved bean cooking liquid (or water) and cover. Bring to a boil and stir in the remaining ½ teaspoon salt. Lower the heat and cook, partially covered, until the squash is tender, about 10 minutes. Stir in the corn and beans and cook, uncovered, an additional 5 minutes to marry the flavors and thicken the filling. Taste and add a pinch more salt if necessary. Set aside while you make the polenta.

Have ready an oiled 8 x 11-inch baking pan. Whisk the water with the corn grits, salt, and chili powder in a medium heat-resistant bowl (metal is best). Fill a 4-quart saucepan halfway with water and bring it to a simmer. Cover the bowl with foil and set it over the water so the water level is below the bottom of the bowl. Cook about 40 minutes, until the polenta is thick and stiff. (Alternatively, use a double boiler insert on top of a medium saucepan.)

Stir 3 or 4 times while the polenta cooks, and add water to the saucepan if necessary.

Stir in the butter, if using, when the polenta is ready. Taste and add additional salt if necessary. Ladle 2 cups of the polenta into the baking pan and spread evenly.

Pour the stew on top to make another even layer. Top with the remaining polenta (about 2½ cups) and smooth with an offset spatula. Let cool until room temperature.

You can make it to this point and refrigerate it for up to 2 days.

When you are ready to bake, preheat the oven to 375°F. Score the top layer of polenta into portion-sized pieces. Brush the top with the olive oil.

Bake until the polenta has browned, about 30 minutes. Serve hot, with a dollop of pumpkinseed pesto.

Pumpkinseed Pesto

This green paste packs a lot of flavor and is a must with the casserole.

MAKES 1 CUP

1 cup pumpkinseeds
1 cup coarsely chopped cilantro
½ cup toasted pumpkinseed oil (or substitute extra virgin olive oil)
¼ cup fresh lime juice
1 teaspoon salt
Pinch of cayenne pepper

Dry-toast the pumpkinseeds in a heavy-bottomed skillet until they pop and plump, about 3 minutes. Remove from the heat and transfer the seeds to a food processor along with the cilantro, oil, lime juice, salt, and cayenne. Process until smooth. Taste and add a pinch more salt if necessary. Store in a small container in the refrigerator. Serve at room temperature.

Maple Sugar–Brined Southwestern-Style Turkey

THE SECRET to this moist, flavorful bird is a paste of salt, sugar, and spices that is slipped under the skin and left overnight to infuse the meat with its beautiful and fragrant smokiness.

Cooking the turkey breast side down for the first hour and a half keeps it moist.

It is worth ordering the maple sugar and smoked paprika by mail if you can't get them at a store near you (see Resources, page 251).

SERVES 10 TO 12 WITH PLENTY OF LEFTOVERS

¼ cup maple sugar

4 teaspoons salt

¼ cup dried thyme

2 tablespoons smoked paprika

2 tablespoons ground cumin

2 teaspoons freshly ground black pepper

3 cups water

One 10- to 12-pound turkey, preferably organic, giblets removed

2 tablespoons extra virgin olive oil

Mole Gravy with Dried Plums and Ancho Chiles (recipe follows)

The day before roasting, in a small bowl, mix together the maple sugar, salt, thyme, paprika, cumin, and black pepper. Stir in ¼ cup water to make a paste. With your fingers, rub the mixture all over the turkey. Then use your fingers to loosen the skin over the breast meat and rub the mixture underneath. Place the turkey, breast side down, on a roasting rack over a rimmed baking pan or platter and refrigerate, uncovered, overnight.

One hour before roasting, remove the turkey from the refrigerator and let stand for an hour at room temperature. About 15 to 20 minutes before roasting, position a shelf in the lowest part of the oven and preheat the oven to 350°F.

Brush the back side of the turkey with the oil.

Place the turkey (and rack) in a large roasting pan. Pour 2 cups water into the pan. Roast, breast side down, for 1½ hours. Remove the turkey from the oven. Using silicone gloves, or paper towels, or aluminum foil to protect your hands, turn the bird breast side up.

Return the turkey to the oven. Add ¾ cup water to the roasting pan. Continue roasting, basting occasionally with pan juices, until an instant-read thermometer inserted into the thigh registers 180°F, about 1½ hours for a 10-pound turkey or 2 hours for a 12-pound turkey. Remove the turkey and rack and tent it with foil to keep warm. Let rest at room temperature 30 to 45 minutes before carving. Pour off the pan drippings into a fat separator or pour into a container and freeze for 20 minutes to separate the fat. You should end up with about ½ cup defatted pan drippings for the mole gravy.

Carve the turkey and serve with the mole gravy.

Mole Gravy with Dried Plums and Ancho Chiles

The dried plum (aka prune), ancho chile, and toasted pumpkinseed paste can be made ahead. Once the turkey comes out of the oven, the rest of the gravy goes together quickly. While the drippings from the turkey add rich flavor, a delicious vegetarian variation to go with the Three Sisters Polenta Casserole can be made using roasted vegetable stock and additional spices.

MAKES ABOUT 3 CUPS

Boiling water
4 ancho chiles (2-ounce bag) or 7 guajillo chiles (2-ounce bag), stemmed and seeded
½ cup pumpkinseeds
½ cup pitted prunes
1 tablespoon extra virgin olive oil
Turkey drippings, defatted (about ½ cup)
2 to 2½ cups chicken stock, canned or homemade (page 5)
1 ounce unsweetened chocolate, chopped
Salt

Pour the boiling water over the chiles and let them soften for at least 10 minutes. Meanwhile, dry-toast the pumpkinseeds in a heavy-bottomed skillet until starting to pop, about 3 minutes. Transfer the seeds to a food processor and process to a powder. Drain the chiles and add them along with the prunes. Process to a paste, scraping down the sides from time to time.

Warm the olive oil in a small pot. Add the paste and the turkey drippings and stir to combine. Let the mixture cook for a few minutes, stirring constantly. Gradually stir in the stock until the gravy reaches a desired consistency. Stir in the chocolate and whisk to combine. Season with salt to taste. Store the gravy, refrigerated, for up to 2 weeks.

VARIATION

vegetarian Mole Gravy

MAKES 2 ½ CUPS

Follow the first two steps of the recipe to make the chile-pumpkinseed-prune paste.

Warm the olive oil and ½ teaspoon smoked paprika, ½ teaspoon ground cumin, 1 teaspoon dried thyme, a sprinkling of black pepper, and the paste. Sauté for 2 minutes. Add 2 cups roasted vegetable stock (page 4), stirring until the gravy reaches a smooth pourable consistency. Stir in the chocolate and whisk until melted. Season with salt to taste. You can strain the gravy if you like a smoother texture. Store the gravy, refrigerated, for up to 2 weeks.

Herbed Mushroom and Wild Rice Dressing with Pine Nuts

Wild rice, pine nuts, and flavorful porcini stock lend richness to this variation on a traditional dressing.

You'll need 1 cup cooked wild rice for this recipe, so start with ⅓ cup dry and cook in 3 cups water for 45 to 50 minutes, until tender. Some of the kernels will have burst open. Drain any extra liquid.

SERVES 8

1 ounce dried porcini mushrooms (1 cup)
½ cup pine nuts
2 tablespoons extra virgin olive oil
1½ cups onion, cut into small dice
¾ cup celery, cut into small dice
¾ cup carrots, cut into small dice
4 cups cremini mushrooms, thinly sliced
½ teaspoon salt
4 cups bread cubes, crusts removed, from a sourdough or rustic loaf
1 cup cooked wild rice
1 tablespoon chopped fresh thyme
2 tablespoons chopped fresh sage
Freshly ground black pepper

Place the porcini mushrooms in a small pot with 2 cups water over high heat. When the water boils, turn off the heat and let the mushrooms soak until softened, about 20 minutes. Then, to catch any dirt from the mushrooms, pour the liquid through a cheesecloth or damp paper towel–lined strainer. Reserve the liquid.

Chop the mushrooms into small pieces and set aside. Dry-toast the pine nuts in a heavy-bottomed skillet until golden, about 3 minutes. Set aside.

Warm the oil in a large skillet over medium heat. Add the onion, celery, carrots, and cremini mushrooms, including the reserved porcinis. Stir in the salt and cook until the vegetables have reduced and released their juices, about 20 minutes.

Preheat the oven to 350°F. Oil an 8 x 11-inch baking dish.

Add the bread cubes and rice to the skillet. Add the mushroom-soaking liquid and stir to combine until the bread absorbs all the liquid. Stir in the pine nuts, thyme, sage, and a generous sprinkling of black pepper. Taste and add more salt if necessary.

Bake, covered, in the prepared baking dish for 30 minutes. Uncover and bake an additional 30 minutes, until the dressing is browned. Serve hot.

The dressing can be baked the day before and reheated, covered, in a 350°F oven.

Sweet Potato Gratin with Coconut Milk and Chipotle Chile

JUST HALF a chipotle chile gives a beautiful smokiness to this satisfying dish. The coconut milk, which cooks into the potatoes, is both rich and subtle.

Chipotle chiles in adobo sauce are readily available canned at many markets. Once they are opened, store the remainder refrigerated in a covered container for up to 4 months.

SERVES 8

3 pounds sweet potatoes (about 6 medium), peeled and cut into 1/4-inch rounds

One 15-ounce can unsweetened coconut milk

1/2 chipotle chile in adobo sauce, seeded and minced

1 tablespoon fresh lime juice

1 teaspoon salt

1 tablespoon maple syrup

3 garlic cloves, thinly sliced

Preheat the oven to 350°F. In a medium bowl, mix together the sweet potatoes, coconut milk, chipotle chile, lime juice, salt, maple syrup, and garlic. Transfer the mixture to a baking dish (8 x 11-inch Pyrex is ideal). Cover with aluminum foil. Bake 45 minutes to 1 hour, until the sweet potatoes are just tender. Uncover and bake an additional 30 minutes, or until the tops are browned.

Cranberry-Persimmon Sauce with Ginger

COLORFUL PERSIMMONS brighten this cranberry sauce. Buy your persimmons a few days ahead so that they can ripen. The softer the persimmons are, the more delicious they taste, but you don't need perfectly pulpy persimmons to enjoy this recipe.

You can also dice a peeled quince or Asian pear into ¼-inch pieces and substitute in place of the persimmons.

MAKES 3 ¼ CUPS

2 Hachiya persimmons, pulp removed and roughly chopped
    (approximately 1 ¼ cups)
2 tablespoons minced fresh ginger
One 12-ounce bag fresh cranberries (3 cups)
½ cup dried cranberries
2 cups apple cider
¾ cup sugar, preferably evaporated cane sugar
Pinch of salt

Put the persimmons, ginger, fresh and dried cranberries, cider, sugar, and salt in a medium pot. Cover and bring to a boil. Uncover and simmer rapidly until the mixture has reduced, thickened, and become saucy, about 45 minutes. Transfer to a bowl and cool to room temperature. The sauce can be made and refrigerated up to a week in advance. Serve at room temperature.

Beer-Braised Brussels Sprouts

LARGE BRUSSELS SPROUTS, cut in half, caramelize beautifully and soak up the flavors of the mustard and honey.

SERVES 8

1¼ pounds brussels sprouts (two 10-ounce packages)
3 tablespoons honey
1 tablespoon Dijon mustard
2 tablespoons extra virgin olive oil
¾ cup beer
¼ teaspoon salt
Freshly ground black pepper
2 tablespoons butter (optional)

Slice off the hard stems of the brussels sprouts, leaving enough root end to keep them intact. Cut in half.

Whisk the honey and mustard together in a small bowl and set aside.

Warm the oil in a large skillet over medium-high heat. Add the sprouts, cut-side down, and sauté until browned, about 2 to 3 minutes. Add the beer and honey-mustard mixture to the pan along with the salt. Lower the heat to medium, cover, and cook for about 8 to 10 minutes, until the sprouts are tender. Uncover and cook at a rapid simmer, stirring occasionally, until the liquid reduces and forms a glaze, about 5 minutes.

Sprinkle with black pepper.

Melt the butter, if using, in a small pot until nutty and golden, 2 to 3 minutes. Drizzle over the sprouts. Serve hot.

Autumn Greens with Pearl Onions

*T*HESE TASTY greens are flavored with smashed garlic, studded with pearl onions, and finished with balsamic vinegar.

SERVES 8

½ pound pearl onions, preferably red

2 tablespoons extra virgin olive oil

I head garlic (about 12 cloves), peeled and smashed

3 to 4 pounds greens (I large bunch collard greens and 2 bunches Swiss chard is a good combination), washed, stemmed, and chopped into bite-sized pieces

½ teaspoon salt

Freshly ground black pepper

½ cup apple cider

2 tablespoons balsamic vinegar

Cut off the tips and root ends of the onions. Bring a small pot of water to a boil and blanch the onions for 1 minute. Drain and remove the papery skins.

Warm the olive oil with the garlic in a large pot over medium-low heat, stirring until the garlic is golden, taking care not to burn it. Remove the garlic and set it aside. Add the onions and sauté until golden, about 7 to 8 minutes. Remove them and set aside.

Add the greens, salt, a sprinkling of black pepper, and the cider. Cook, covered, lifting the lid occasionally to push the uncooked leaves to the bottom with tongs until the greens are almost tender. Stir in the garlic and onions and cook, uncovered, an additional 5 to 10 minutes, until the greens are tender and most of the liquid has evaporated. Stir in the vinegar and serve hot.

Butternut Semifreddo Pie

*H*ERE'S A cool and delicate finale to your Thanksgiving feast. It's the perfect dessert to make ahead. With a gingersnap crust, it looks and tastes a lot like a pumpkin cheesecake but is much lighter in texture. The dessert is frozen, then partially thawed in the refrigerator and served chilled.

MAKES ONE 9-INCH PIE (SERVES 10 TO 12)

One 2-pound butternut squash
One 7-ounce package gingersnaps
3 tablespoons butter, melted
1 teaspoon ground cinnamon
1 teaspoon ground ginger
¼ teaspoon freshly grated nutmeg
¼ teaspoon salt
4 eggs
¾ cup sugar, preferably maple sugar
1 cup heavy cream
⅓ cup crystallized ginger, chopped small

Preheat the oven to 375°F. Cut the squash in half and place it facedown on a parchment-covered baking sheet. Roast the squash until tender, about 40 minutes. Remove from the oven and let cool. Lower the heat to 350°F.

Process the gingersnaps in a food processor until you have crumbs. You should have about 1 cup. Transfer them to a small bowl.

Melt the butter in a small pot. Stir the butter into the gingersnaps and toss to moisten. Press the crust evenly into a 9-inch springform pan. Bake for 15 minutes, until firm. Remove from the oven and let cool.

Remove and discard the seeds from the squash. Scoop the flesh into a food processor and purée until smooth. You should have 2 cups. If you have more, set aside the extra for another use.

Combine 2 cups squash purée with the cinnamon, ginger, nutmeg, and salt in a small pot and heat, stirring constantly, until the squash is heated through and the spices cook a bit, about 3 to 4 minutes.

Use the bowl of your stand mixer or another heatproof bowl and whisk together the eggs with the sugar by hand. (This way you won't have to change bowls.) Set the bowl over a pot of simmering water (make sure the bottom of the bowl does not touch the water), and whisk gently and thoroughly, scraping the bottom frequently, until the liquid is hot to the touch (about 160°F on an instant-read thermometer). Remove the bowl from the heat and reattach it to the stand mixer. Beat the eggs at high speed with the whisk attachment to the consistency of softly whipped cream, about 5 minutes.

Pour the squash into a medium bowl. Stir one-fourth of the egg mixture into the squash, then fold in the rest of the egg mixture, one-third at a time, until no streaks remain.

Whip the cream in the stand mixer until soft peaks form, about 3 to 4 minutes. Fold into the squash and egg mixture.

Pour the filling into the crust. Sprinkle with the crystallized ginger. Place the semifreddo in the freezer and freeze until solid, about 2 to 4 hours.

To serve, remove the springform and cut the semifreddo into portions while frozen. Refrigerate the slices 1 to 2 hours before serving to get the perfect texture.

Pear and Apple Pie with Cranberries

YOUR KITCHEN will smell great even before your pie hits the oven. Sautéed apples, sliced pears, and cranberries make a delectable and mysterious combination. The cranberries are subtle, melting into a beautiful burgundy, and the pears give it depth of flavor. This is sure to become a holiday favorite.

Some wonderful autumnal varieties of apples to use include Ida Red, Winesap, Cortland, Mutsu, Rome Beauty, Northern Spy, and Jonagold. A combination of Golden Delicious and Granny Smith is fine too.

MAKES ONE 9-INCH PIE (SERVES 10)

2 pounds apples (about 4 to 6 medium apples)
4 tablespoons butter or 3 tablespoons coconut oil
1¼ cups plus 1 teaspoon maple sugar or evaporated cane sugar (see page 8)
2 pounds semifirm pears (about 4), Anjou, Bartlett, or red
1 cup cranberries
Pinch of salt
2 teaspoons ground cinnamon
¾ teaspoon allspice
2 teaspoons freshly grated lemon zest
1 tablespoon lemon juice
3 tablespoons unbleached white flour
1 double crust recipe (page 50 or page 51)

Peel and core the apples. Cut each quarter into 4 lengthwise slices.

Melt the butter or oil in a large skillet. Add the apples and ½ cup of the sugar and cook over medium-high heat, stirring frequently, until the apples are caramelized and tender (do not overcook), 6 to 7 minutes. Remove from the heat and transfer to a large bowl.

Peel, core, and quarter the pears. Cut each quarter into thin slices, no thicker than ¼ inch. Toss with the cooked apples.

Pulse the cranberries in the food processor to break them up and add the chunky pieces to the pears along with ¾ cup of the sugar, the salt, cinnamon, allspice, lemon zest, and lemon juice. Sprinkle the flour over the top and stir to combine. Set the mixture aside while rolling out the dough.

Preheat the oven to 350°F. Have ready a 9-inch pie plate. Start with one ball of dough. On a lightly floured board or between 2 pieces of parchment paper, roll out the dough. Start from the center and move outward in all directions, rolling the dough until it is as thin as possible (about ¹/₁₆ inch). Transfer the dough to the 9-inch pie plate.

Lightly push in the crust to meet the contours of the pie pan. Leave the overhang for now.

Add the filling to the crust, neatly mounding it in. Roll out the second crust in the same way as the first and center it over the pie. Trim the 2 crusts together around the edge of the pie plate using a small knife or a kitchen scissors. Pinch the 2 crusts together. Make a decorative edge by pressing a piece of the dough in between the forefinger of one hand and the thumb and forefinger of the other hand. Repeat this motion to create a zigzag pattern around the rim of the pie.

Make 5 or 6 slashes in the top crust to allow steam to escape while baking. At this point, you can freeze the pie for up to 3 weeks.

Brush the top crust with water and sprinkle the remaining teaspoon of sugar over the top. Bake about 1 hour, until the crust is golden brown and you can see the juices bubbling. Remove from the oven and let cool to room temperature before cutting. Serve warm or at room temperature.

Double Crust with Butter

*T*HIS IS a great all-purpose whole grain butter crust. Making your own piecrust takes just seconds in a food processor.

You can make the dough up to 2 days in advance and keep it in the refrigerator, or you can freeze the dough for up to a month. After you refrigerate the dough, let it sit for a few minutes before rolling. Depending on the time of year or how cold it is, you may have to give it a couple of whacks with a rolling pin to soften it enough for rolling.

> 1½ cups unbleached white flour
> 1 cup whole wheat pastry flour
> 1 teaspoon baking powder
> ¼ cup maple sugar, Sucanat, or evaporated cane sugar (see page 8)
> ½ teaspoon salt
> 1½ sticks unsalted butter, chilled, cut into small cubes
> 2 teaspoons apple cider vinegar
> 7 tablespoons ice water

Place the flours, baking powder, sugar, and salt in the bowl of a food processor. Process for a couple of seconds to combine. Add the butter and pulse until the flour and butter become crumbs, about 7 to 10 pulses. The crumbs should be uneven, but none should be larger than the size of small pebbles.

Stir the vinegar into the water, add to the crumbs, and pulse for a couple of seconds until just combined. Do not process until the dough becomes a ball.

Remove the dough from the bowl and gather into a ball. With the heel of your hand, press the dough onto a board to bind together. Form into two 4-inch disks. Wrap the disks in plastic wrap and chill in the refrigerator for at least 1 hour. Let sit at room temperature for 10 to 15 minutes to soften before rolling out.

Double Crust with Coconut Oil

*H*ERE'S A delicious dairy-free alternative to the butter crust. Scoop out some of the coconut oil, place it in the refrigerator, and measure it after it firms up. Chill the dough only 5 minutes before rolling out.

    1½ cups unbleached white flour
    1 cup whole wheat pastry flour
    1 teaspoon baking powder
    ¼ cup maple sugar, Sucanat, or evaporated cane sugar (see page 8)
    ½ teaspoon salt
    ¾ cup coconut oil, chilled until solid
    2 teaspoons apple cider vinegar
    10 to 12 tablespoons ice water

Place the flours, baking powder, sugar, and salt in the bowl of a food processor. Process for a couple of seconds to combine.

Remove the coconut oil from the refrigerator. If you chop it up on the cutting board into pebble-sized pieces before filling the measuring cup, it will be easy to measure. Add the coconut oil to the work bowl of the food processor and pulse for about 15 seconds until the coconut oil is coated and the mixture is crumbly like wet sand.

Pour the mixture out into a bowl. Add the cider vinegar to the ice water. Drizzle the water into the dough a spoonful at a time, tossing lightly as you go. You have enough water in the dough when the dough holds together when squeezed. Do not add any more water than is absolutely necessary.

Gather the dough into a ball. Divide the dough into 2 balls and wrap each ball in plastic. Refrigerate for about 5 minutes before rolling out.

chanukah

CHANUKAH IS A JOYFUL Jewish holiday that takes place for eight days starting on the twenty-fifth of Kislev on the Jewish calendar, usually sometime in December. Known as the Festival of Lights, Chanukah is a time of family gatherings, singing, gift giving, and of course, feasting. Foods cooked in oil are traditional, and potato pancakes, known as latkes, are consumed throughout the holiday.

The holiday commemorates the Maccabean uprising that took place more than twenty-one centuries ago. After three years of fighting, a small band of faithful Jews defeated the mighty armies of Antiochus II, a ruler who had sought to Hellenize the people of Israel by force. After driving their oppressors from the land, the Jews set out to purify and sanctify the holy temple. They found only a tiny amount of holy oil, which miraculously lasted an entire week, enough time to make a new batch.

Creating light to commemorate the miracle is a focal point of the holiday: The home serves as a temple, and lighting the menorah symbolizes illuminating darkness and ignorance with wisdom and harmony. Arthur Waskow states in *Seasons of Our Joy* that "Chanukah is the moment when light is born from darkness, hope from despair."

Other celebratory activities include spinning a top called a dreidel, each surface with a letter that stands for the first initial of each word in the phrase "A great miracle happened there."

The ultimate comfort food, potato latkes have a particularly colorful history. The story goes that Judith, an exceedingly beautiful and brave woman, used her seductive charms to avert disaster to her hometown. She lured the Assyrian general Holofernes to sleep and to his demise after feeding him salty cheeses and copious amounts of strong wine. In memory of Judith, cheese became a traditional food consumed on the holiday. The original latkes made by the Sephardic Jews of the Middle East were cheese pancakes. Because of the scarcity of dairy products in Eastern Europe during winter, Ashkenazic Jews substituted potatoes for the customary cheese.

Since we have access to lots of wonderful vegetables, I opt for a "latkemania" party featuring a colorful variety. Oil is venerated on Chanukah, and some, including my former neighbors, go as far as to finish a meal of potato latkes with fried doughnuts. I am of the opinion that latkes are much more enjoyable if they are not too heavy or greasy, so the recipes here are for light and flavorful pancakes. The root vegetable latkes are steamed for just a couple of minutes to take the raw edge off, and then mixed with some flavorings and cooked in a small amount of oil. The resulting savory parsnip, sweet potato, and celery root pancakes make great vegetable side dishes. Also included are traditional potato and zucchini-cheese varieties and a bright green spinach latke with a coconut crust. The Mulled Cider–Cranberry Applesauce is delicious on all of the latkes, and it makes a great Thanksgiving relish. A soup, salad, and Double Chocolate Cloud Cookies round out the feast. The pancakes all freeze beautifully, leaving you able to enjoy the party without spending lots of time at the stove at the last minute.

Cook's Notes

Up to 2 weeks before:

Make an all-purpose vegetable, roasted vegetable, or chicken stock.
Make any or all of the pancakes and freeze them.

3 days before:

Make the Mulled Cider–Cranberry Applesauce.
Roast the squash and shallots for the soup.

2 days before:

Make the soup.

Day before:

Drain the yogurt.

Make the fennel-orange walnut salad.

Make the cookie batter and store in the refrigerator.

Day of:

Bake the cookies.

Add the parsley to the salad.

Make the shallot cream.

Rewarm the chickpeas.

Rewarm the latkes and heat the soup.

You can also make the latkes the day of the party and leave them covered at room temperature. Pop them in a 350°F oven to heat through.

Golden Squash and Chickpea Soup with Roasted Chickpea Nuts

THIS COMFORTING soup is flavored with ginger, coriander, and fresh thyme and topped with roasted chickpeas. Plump chickpeas shrink and tighten as they roast and end up crispy and nutlike. To save time, roast them on a second tray along with the squash and shallots, and be sure to make extra to snack on.

While the soup is extra delicious with roasted vegetable or chicken stock, a simple vegetable stock or even water yields fine results.

SERVES 6 TO 8

One 2½-pound butternut squash
4 shallots, unpeeled
2 tablespoons extra virgin olive oil
2 cups chopped leeks, white and light green parts only
1 garlic clove, minced
1 tablespoon minced ginger
1 teaspoon ground coriander
2 tablespoons chopped fresh thyme
One 15-ounce can chickpeas, drained and rinsed (or 1½ cups cooked chickpeas)
6 to 7 cups roasted vegetable, chicken, or vegetable stock, canned or homemade (pages 4, 5, or 6)
1½ teaspoons salt, plus additional for seasoning
Freshly ground black pepper
1 tablespoon fresh lemon juice
1 recipe chickpea nuts (page 58)

Preheat the oven to 375°F. Cut the squash in half and place facedown in a parchment-covered baking dish along with the whole shallots. Place in the oven and bake until tender, about 45 minutes. Remove from the oven and set aside to cool.

Squeeze the shallots out of their skins and set aside. Remove and discard the seeds from the squash. Scrape out the flesh and set aside. You should have 3 cups.

(continued)

Meanwhile, in a medium pot, warm the oil with the leeks and sweat over medium-low heat, about 10 minutes, until softened. Add the garlic, ginger, coriander, and 1 tablespoon of the thyme and cook for 1 minute. Stir in the chickpeas, squash, shallots, 6 cups stock, and salt. Cover and bring to a boil. Reduce the heat and simmer 15 minutes to marry the flavors.

Use a handheld blender or transfer the soup to a stand blender and blend until smooth. Return the soup to the pot, sprinkle with black pepper, and stir in the lemon juice. Thin out the soup with the remaining cup of stock if necessary. Taste and add additional salt if desired. Serve hot, garnished with the chickpea nuts and the remaining tablespoon thyme.

Chickpea Nuts

In a medium bowl, toss one 15-ounce can drained and rinsed chickpeas (or 1½ cups cooked) with 1 tablespoon extra virgin olive oil, 1 tablespoon fresh lemon juice, a large pinch of cayenne, and ½ teaspoon salt. Spread on a parchment-covered baking sheet and roast in a 375°F oven for about 45 minutes, stirring 2 or 3 times, until the chickpeas are shrunken and browned. Remove from the oven and sprinkle lightly with salt. Store refrigerated in a covered container. Place on a baking tray in a 350°F oven for 10 minutes to rewarm.

MAKES 1½ CUPS

Winter Citrus Salad with Parsley, Fennel, and Walnuts

THIS JUICY salad, with its refreshing combination of flavors and textures, is a wonderful complement to the latkes.

Soaking onion in water mutes its sulfuric compounds, taking away its harsh bite. If you make the salad in advance, stir in the parsley the day you are serving it.

SERVES 4

I cup red onion, thinly sliced into halved rings
4 navel oranges or tangerines
I medium fennel bulb
¼ cup olives, preferably kalamata, halved, or niçoise, whole (optional)
I cup chopped fresh parsley
½ teaspoon salt
Freshly ground black pepper
2 tablespoons extra virgin olive oil
½ cup walnuts
I bunch watercress, washed, with hard stems removed
¼ pound feta cheese, preferably sheep's milk, crumbled, about ¾ cup (optional)

Soak the onion in cold water for 15 minutes. Drain and dry thoroughly.

Cut the peel and any white pith from the oranges with a sharp paring knife, then cut the sections free from the membranes, letting them drop into a medium bowl to collect the juices, which will become part of the dressing. Add the onions to the citrus.

Trim the fennel, using a peeler to peel off any discolored parts. Halve the fennel and cut away the hard core. Using a mandoline or a knife, slice the fennel halves very thinly and add it to the citrus along with the olives. If you plan to serve this immediately, stir in the parsley at this point as well. Stir in the salt and sprinkle with black pepper. Stir in the olive oil and let sit for 30 minutes or so to let the flavors marry.

In a medium, heavy-bottomed skillet, dry-toast the walnuts until fragrant, about 5 minutes. Rub the walnuts against the strainer (over the sink or wastebasket) to loosen the skins. Remove the walnuts from the strainer and chop into small (¼-inch) pieces.

Serve the salad on the watercress, sprinkled with the walnuts and cheese.

Making and Storing the Latkes

For ease in preparation, grate the vegetables on the grating blade of your food processor. Use the large holes on a box grater if you are grating the vegetables by hand.

The root vegetables are steamed for just a couple of minutes to take the raw edge off before they are mixed with seasonings and cooked in a small amount of oil. The resulting savory potato, parsnip, sweet potato, and celery root pancakes make great accompaniments to just about anything.

All of the latkes, including the spinach and zucchini-cheese, can be made in advance and freeze beautifully. To freeze, lay the pancakes in a single layer on a baking sheet for an hour or so until frozen. Then stack and store in freezer bags. To defrost, lay the pancakes out in a single layer on a baking sheet and defrost at room temperature for 15 minutes. Rewarm in a 350°F oven for 15 minutes, or until heated through.

Parsnip Latkes with Leeks and Thyme

THE PARSNIP'S rich and buttery flavor is complemented by the leek, red onion, and thyme.

MAKES 12 TO 14 PANCAKES

1 pound parsnips, peeled

1 cup leek, finely diced, white and light green parts only

½ cup minced red onion

2 tablespoons minced fresh thyme

1 egg, lightly beaten

6 tablespoons unbleached white flour

1 teaspoon salt

Freshly ground black pepper

Extra virgin olive oil or coconut oil, for frying

Preheat the oven to 200°F.

Grate the parsnips, using the grating blade on a food processor or the large holes on a box grater. You should have about 6 cups. Steam for 2 minutes, until just tender and slightly moistened. Transfer to a bowl and stir in the leek, onion, thyme, egg, flour, salt, and a generous sprinkling of black pepper.

Form a heaping tablespoon of batter into a patty by hand. (Do not overwork.) Repeat with the remaining batter to make 12 to 14 latkes. Place them on a large plate.

Warm a thin layer of oil over medium-high heat in a large, heavy-bottomed or nonstick skillet until it feels hot when your hand is held 1 inch above the pan. Lay 4 or 5 latkes in the oil, being careful not to overcrowd the pan. Cook until golden, about 4 minutes.

Flip to the other side, pressing down the patties with a spatula to flatten slightly. Cook until golden, another 2 minutes or so. Continue with the remaining latkes, adding more oil to the pan between batches as necessary. Spread on a baking sheet and keep warm in the oven until you are ready to serve.

Sweet Potato—Turnip Latkes

TURNIPS ADD just enough bite to take the sweet edge off and give these latkes a sophisticated flavor.

MAKES TWELVE 4-INCH-DIAMETER PANCAKES

1 pound sweet potatoes (2 medium or 1 large)
½ pound turnips (1 medium)
½ cup minced shallots
1 teaspoon salt
Freshly ground black pepper
1 egg
6 tablespoons unbleached white flour
Extra virgin olive oil or coconut oil, for frying

Preheat the oven to 200°F.

Peel the sweet potatoes and turnips. Grate the vegetables, using the grating blade on a food processor or the large holes on a box grater. You should have about 6 cups.

Steam the vegetables for 2 minutes, until just tender and slightly moistened. Transfer to a medium bowl. Add the shallots, salt, and a sprinkling of black pepper. Stir in the egg and flour.

Form a heaping tablespoon of batter into a patty by hand. (Do not overwork.) Repeat with the remaining batter to make 12 latkes. Place them on a large plate.

Warm a thin layer of oil over medium-high heat in a large, heavy-bottomed or nonstick skillet until it feels hot when your hand is held 1 inch above the pan. Lay 4 or 5 latkes in the oil, being careful not to overcrowd the pan. Cook until golden, about 4 minutes.

Flip to the other side, pressing down the patties with a spatula to flatten slightly. Cook until golden, another 2 minutes or so. Continue with the remaining latkes, adding more oil to the pan between batches as necessary. Spread on a baking sheet and keep warm in the oven until you are ready to serve.

Celery Root–Apple Latkes with Sage

SAGE AND green apples harmonize with the celery-like taste of this underappreciated root vegetable.

MAKES 12 PANCAKES

I pound celery root, peeled
1/2 pound (1 large) Granny Smith apple, peeled
I tablespoon minced fresh sage
1/2 cup minced red onion
I teaspoon salt
Freshly ground black pepper
I egg
6 tablespoons unbleached white flour
Extra virgin olive or coconut oil, for frying

Preheat the oven to 200°F.

Grate the celery root and apple, using the grating blade on a food processor or the large holes on a box grater. Steam for 2 minutes, until just tender and slightly moistened. Transfer to a bowl and stir in the sage, onion, salt, a sprinkling of black pepper, the egg, and the flour.

Form a heaping tablespoon of batter into a patty by hand. (Do not overwork.) Repeat with the remaining batter to make 12 latkes. Place them on a large plate.

Warm a thin layer of oil over medium-high heat in a large, heavy-bottomed or nonstick skillet until it feels hot when your hand is held 1 inch above the pan. Lay 4 or 5 latkes in the oil, being careful not to overcrowd the pan. Cook until golden, about 4 minutes.

Flip to the other side, pressing down the patties with a spatula to flatten slightly. Cook until golden, another 2 minutes or so. Continue with the remaining latkes, adding more oil to the pan between batches as necessary. Spread on a baking sheet and keep warm in the oven until you are ready to serve.

Potato Latkes

*T*HE CLASSIC, only lighter.

MAKES **20** PANCAKES

1½ pounds russet potatoes (2 to 3 large), peeled
½ pound carrots, peeled
½ cup thinly sliced scallions, white and green parts
1 cup minced onions
1½ teaspoons salt
6 tablespoons unbleached white flour
1 egg
Freshly ground black pepper
Extra virgin olive oil or coconut oil, for frying

Preheat the oven to 200°F.

Grate the potatoes, using the grating blade on a food processor or the large holes on a box grater. Steam for 4 minutes, until just softened and slightly moistened. Grate the carrots separately. Transfer the potatoes to a large bowl and add the carrots, scallions, onions, salt, flour, egg, and a sprinkling of black pepper.

Form a heaping tablespoon of batter into a patty by hand. (Do not overwork.) Repeat with the remaining batter to make 20 latkes. Place them on a large plate.

Warm a thin layer of oil over medium-high heat in a large, heavy-bottomed or nonstick skillet until it feels hot when your hand is held 1 inch above the pan. Lay 4 or 5 latkes in the oil, being careful not to overcrowd the pan. Cook until golden, about 4 minutes.

Flip to the other side, pressing down the patties with a spatula to flatten slightly. Cook until golden, another 2 minutes or so. Continue with the remaining latkes, adding more oil to the pan between batches as necessary. Spread on a baking sheet and keep warm in the oven until you are ready to serve.

cheese pancakes with zucchini and walnuts

CHEESE PANCAKES were traditional before potatoes became the standard. The uncooked mixture for these latkes is looser than the other batters, and the resulting pancakes are extraordinarily light and creamy.

These make a scrumptious breakfast pancake too.

MAKES 18 TO 20 PANCAKES

½ pound zucchini (2 small)
½ teaspoon salt
3 eggs
1 cup ricotta cheese (½ pound)
1 cup feta cheese, crumbled (6 ounces)
½ cup grated onion
½ cup walnuts, toasted and chopped
¼ cup unbleached white flour
¼ teaspoon baking powder
Freshly ground black pepper
Extra virgin olive oil or coconut oil, for frying

Preheat the oven to 200°F.

Grate the zucchini, using the grating blade on a food processor or the large holes on a box grater. Sprinkle with the salt, stir to combine, and let sit for 30 minutes in a strainer or colander positioned over a bowl. Then grab handfuls of the zucchini and squeeze out the water. Do this twice on each handful to squeeze out as much liquid as possible. Transfer the zucchini to a small bowl.

In a medium bowl, whisk together the eggs until frothy. Stir in the ricotta cheese and beat until well combined. Stir in the feta cheese, onions, walnuts, flour, baking powder, and a generous sprinkling of black pepper. Stir in the zucchini.

With a paper towel, lightly oil a large nonstick skillet or griddle and heat over a medium flame. In batches, drop 2 tablespoons of the batter on the griddle and cook until bubbles form on the tops and the bottoms are lightly brown, 2 to 3 minutes. Flip the pancakes and use your spatula to flatten them. Cook on the second side until golden, 1 to 2 minutes more. Add oil between batches, using a paper towel to spread thinly. The pancakes may be kept warm by placing in a single layer on a baking sheet in the oven. Serve hot.

Coconut-Crusted Spinach Pancakes with Basil

THESE ARE exotic and exciting latkes. A crispy, golden coconut crust conceals an unexpected, bright green herbed spinach pancake.

MAKES 10 PANCAKES

1½ pounds spinach, washed, with stems removed
½ cup finely chopped fresh basil
¼ cup finely chopped fresh cilantro
1 tablespoon minced fresh ginger
¼ cup unbleached white flour
1 egg, lightly beaten
1 teaspoon salt
Freshly ground black pepper
1 cup dried, unsweetened coconut
Extra virgin olive oil or coconut oil, for frying

Preheat the oven to 200°F.

Wilt the spinach in a large skillet over medium heat, stirring frequently or tossing with tongs to push the uncooked leaves to the bottom of the pot. You don't have to add water to the pot because the water clinging to the leaves from washing is enough to cook them.

Cook until the leaves have wilted, shrunk, and are bright green. Remove and place in a strainer. Squeeze against the strainer to remove any excess water, then place on a cutting board and chop finely.

Transfer to a medium bowl and stir in the basil, cilantro, ginger, flour, egg, salt, and a sprinkling of black pepper.

Mix to combine well.

Spread the coconut onto a plate. In the bowl, divide the spinach mixture into 10 portions. With a spoon, drop each portion onto the coconut. Sprinkle the top with coconut to make it easy to handle, and form into patties with your hands. Place them on a large plate.

Warm a thin layer of oil over medium-high heat in a large, heavy-bottomed or nonstick skillet. When the oil is hot (test by placing your hand 1 inch above the skillet), lay 4 or 5 latkes in the oil, being careful not to overcrowd the pan. Cook until golden, about 4 minutes. Flip to the other side, pressing down the patties with a spatula to flatten slightly. Cook another 2 minutes or so, until golden. Continue with the remaining latkes, adding more oil to the pan between batches as necessary. Spread on a baking sheet and keep warm in the oven until you are ready to serve.

Thickened Yogurt with Caramelized Shallots

THICKENED YOGURT is a luscious alternative to the traditional sour cream. Caramelized shallots add a rich onion flavor, making this garnish more satisfying than the original.

Drain your own yogurt or use thick Greek-style yogurt. The tofu version (page 68) is great for those who don't eat dairy.

MAKES 1 CUP

2 cups plain yogurt
2 tablespoons extra virgin olive oil
1/2 cup shallots, cut into thin rings
Salt

Place the yogurt in a cheesecloth-lined strainer over a bowl. Let the yogurt drain in the refrigerator for at least 2 hours or, if it's more convenient, through the night. Two cups yogurt will become about 1 cup thickened.

Warm the oil in a medium nonstick skillet. Add the shallots and cook over medium heat for about 5 minutes, stirring frequently to cook evenly, until they are browned and crispy.

Immediately stir the shallots into the yogurt, along with any remaining oil. Sprinkle with salt and serve with the latkes. Store, covered, in the refrigerator for up to 2 days.

Tofu Cream with Caramelized Shallots

MAKES 1 CUP

½ pound silken tofu
2 tablespoons fresh lemon juice
2 teaspoons brown rice vinegar
¾ teaspoon salt
2 tablespoons extra virgin olive oil
½ cup shallots, cut into thin rings

Put the tofu, lemon juice, vinegar, and salt in a food processor and process until creamy. Place the mixture in a small bowl.

Warm the oil in a medium nonstick skillet. Add the shallots and cook over medium heat for about 5 minutes, stirring frequently to cook evenly, until the shallots are browned and crispy.

Immediately stir into the tofu cream, along with any remaining oil. Serve dolloped on the latkes. Store, covered, in the refrigerator for up to 2 days.

Mulled Cider–Cranberry Applesauce

*W*ARMING SPICES and mulled cider make this rosy sauce the perfect accompaniment to all of the latkes. Be sure to try it on the spinach too.

It also makes a great Thanksgiving relish.

MAKES 4 CUPS

I navel orange
10 whole cloves
4 cups apple cider
2 cinnamon sticks
¼ teaspoon ground allspice
I pound apples, preferably McIntosh, peeled and cut into ¾-inch pieces (3 cups)
One 12-ounce bag cranberries (3 cups)
½ cup sugar, preferably maple or evaporated cane sugar

Stud the orange with the cloves, clustering them together on one side. Place the orange, clove side down, in a medium pot. Add the apple cider, cinnamon sticks, and allspice. Bring to a boil and simmer rapidly, uncovered, until reduced by half, about 20 minutes.

Remove the orange and add the apples, cranberries, and sugar. Simmer, uncovered, stirring from time to time, until the cranberries and apples have melded, about 45 minutes. Remove and discard the cinnamon sticks. Let the sauce cool to room temperature and serve.

Store in the refrigerator for up to 1 week.

Double Chocolate Cloud Cookies

THESE ARE rich cookies with a wonderful trufflelike consistency. They are so light, you would never know they are made with whole grain flour. Use your favorite chocolate and a natural brown sugar like maple, Sucanat, or muscovado.

MAKES 30 COOKIES

6 ounces bittersweet chocolate, chopped

1 stick unsalted butter, at room temperature, or 6 tablespoons coconut oil, at room temperature

1/2 cup whole wheat pastry flour

2 tablespoons unsweetened cocoa powder

1/4 teaspoon baking powder

1/2 teaspoon salt

3/4 cup sugar, preferably natural sugar such as maple or Sucanat

3 eggs

1 1/2 teaspoons vanilla extract

1 cup semisweet chocolate chips

Melt the chopped chocolate and the butter or oil in a small heavy pot or saucepan over low heat, stirring occasionally. Remove from the heat and let cool.

Sift together the flour, cocoa, baking powder, and salt in a medium bowl.

Beat together the sugar, eggs, and vanilla in a stand mixer fitted with the paddle on medium-high speed until pale and fluffy, about 3 to 4 minutes.

Mix in the melted chocolate mixture and then the flour mixture at low speed until well combined, scraping the sides and bottom. Stir in the chocolate chips. Chill, covered, until firm, about 1 hour.

Preheat the oven to 350°F.

Drop well-rounded teaspoons of batter (use 2 spoons to help you) spaced 2 inches apart on a parchment or silicone-covered baking sheet. Bake on the center rack until puffed and set, about 10 minutes (the cookies will be soft in the center). Transfer to racks to cool. Store, covered, at room temperature.

christmas Eve

CHRISTMAS, THE CELEBRATION of the nativity of Jesus Christ on December 25, is the most eagerly anticipated and elaborately celebrated holiday in the United States. The Christmas season begins immediately after Thanksgiving and extends to Epiphany on January 6. Feasting, gift giving, partying, card sending, caroling, relaxing with friends and family, and attending services are some of the ways in which Christmas is typically celebrated. Coming just after the middle of winter when the days are beginning to grow longer, Christmas is a time to forget about the long dark days and celebrate with family and friends.

The actual date of the holiday was set in Rome in A.D. 336 to coincide roughly with the Roman holiday of Saturnalia, the winter solstice. The church was having a hard time burying pagan midwinter traditions, so it absorbed them into the holiday. Kissing under the mistletoe, for instance, probably comes from association with the Scandinavian goddess of love, Frigga.

Over the years the holiday has morphed and changed. Twelfth Night, or Epiphany, the day the magi are said to have visited baby Jesus with gifts, was more popular than Christmas itself from the Middle Ages through the early part of the nineteenth century and remains the central focus in many cultures. Although its importance as a festive holiday has ebbed and flowed over the years, many of the familiar traditions of the modern American Christmas have their roots in the Victorian era.

Of course, with the remarkable diversity of heritages in America, Christmas celebrations vary widely. Feasts range from Creole gumbo in Louisiana to New England lumberjack pie. Eastern European food customs are especially powerful and rich, so I've opted for an Eastern European, mostly Polish-inspired Christmas Eve. In the Eastern European tradition, the big feast and the exchange of gifts takes place on the twenty-fourth of December. An empty place at the dinner table is set for an unexpected guest because, according to Polish folklore, a guest in the home is God in the home. The feast cannot begin until the first star appears in the sky, because it represents the star of Bethlehem, which was said to have guided the magi to the newborn king.

While a variety of dishes may appear on a Polish Christmas table, some families make twelve dishes representing the twelve apostles and expect everyone to try everything. The idea is that the more you eat, the more pleasure awaits you in the future. Foods are selected to represent the four corners of the earth: mushrooms from the forest, grain from the fields, fruit from the orchards, and fish from the lakes and sea.

In the feast presented here, there's the requisite *kutia*, a ritual food that is a mixture of wheat berries, poppy seeds, honey, and walnuts. I've used spelt, an unhybridized form of wheat, since the texture is especially pleasing. The Wild Mushroom, Barley, and Lima Bean Soup is rich and earthy. Three kinds of pierogis, complete with essential accompaniments, are the centerpiece of the meal. I like to make lots of these, so I have extras in the freezer, ready to pop into boiling water for an instant cozy supper. A lemon-baked trout is sprinkled with dill. A brilliant-colored zesty beet and horseradish relish and a refreshing crunchy salad of cauliflower, green beans, and pickles round out the meal. Cheese blintzes topped with a crimson fruit compote make a festive finale to the feast. All of these dishes lend themselves to convenient entertaining, so make this cozy meal for Christmas Eve or any of your midwinter get-togethers.

Cook's Notes

2 weeks before:

Make the pierogi fillings.
Next day, make the dough and fill and freeze the pierogis.

3 days before:

Make the cheese blintzes and freeze.
Make the compote topping and refrigerate.

2 days before:

Make the applesauce.
Make the beet relish.

Day before:

Make the Cauliflower Green Bean Salad with Pickles.
Soak the spelt berries.
Soak the barley and lima beans.

Day of:

Make the soup.
Make the Kutia.
Prepare the trout with the herbed crust.
Caramelize the onions for the pierogis.
Bake the blintzes.

Last minute:

Cook the pierogis.
Bake the trout.

Kutia

*T*HE MOST important food of the entire Polish and Ukrainian Christmas Eve supper, kutia is a first course of boiled wheat berries sweetened with honey and flavored with poppy seeds and nuts. Everyone partakes of a little to ensure prosperity for the coming year.

I've opted for spelt, an unhybridized form of wheat, in place of wheat berries, since it makes an especially tender kutia.

MAKES 3 CUPS (SERVES 9 TO 12)

1 cup spelt berries
½ teaspoon salt
2 tablespoons evaporated cane sugar
¼ cup honey
⅓ cup poppy seeds, ground in a spice grinder or blender
½ cup raisins, soaked in water 5 minutes to plump
½ cup walnuts, toasted and finely chopped

Soak the spelt berries overnight in a medium pot with 6 cups water. In the morning, place on the heat, cover, and bring to a boil. Lower the heat and simmer, partially covered, until most of the berries are tender and splitting open, about 2 to 3 hours. Check from time to time and add more water if necessary, making sure there is always water in the pot. When the berries are cooked, stir in the salt and let sit for 10 minutes. Drain the excess water and let cool.

Place 2 tablespoons water in a small pot along with the sugar. Bring to a boil, stirring, just to dissolve the sugar. Remove from the heat and stir in the honey and poppy seeds. Stir this mixture into the spelt berries along with the raisins. Let cool to room temperature. Stir in the walnuts right before serving. Serve a small amount to start the meal.

Wild Mushroom, Barley, and Lima Bean Soup

*T*HIS DEEP and satisfying winter warmer features mushrooms from the forest and grains from the fields in a rich porcini stock.

For convenience, soak the beans and barley together. Fennel seed usually comes whole, so grind it in a spice grinder or just use the whole seed.

SERVES 6

½ cup dried porcini mushrooms
8 cups water or stock (roasted vegetable [page 4] is especially delicious)
¼ cup barley, semipearled (called hulled in natural foods stores) or pearled, soaked
½ cup large lima beans, soaked (see page 11)
Salt
2 tablespoons extra virgin olive oil
1 cup onion, cut into small dice
1 celery stalk, cut into small dice (½ cup)
4 cups wild mushrooms, such as shiitakes, portobellos, and cremini,
    thinly sliced (½ pound)
1 teaspoon ground fennel seed
1 teaspoon ground coriander seed
1 tablespoon shoyu
¼ cup dry sherry or mirin
¼ cup roughly chopped fresh dill
2 teaspoons fresh lemon juice
Freshly ground black pepper
1 cup fresh or frozen peas

Place the porcinis in a medium pot with 6 cups of the water or stock. Bring the liquid just to a boil, then turn off the heat. Let the mushrooms sit for 20 minutes. Drain, reserving the liquid. Finely chop the mushrooms and set aside. Pour the liquid through a cheese-cloth or paper towel–lined strainer to catch any grit left by the mushrooms.

Drain the barley and lima beans. Pour the reserved and strained liquid from the mushrooms back into the pot along with the barley, lima beans, and ³/₄ teaspoon salt. Bring to a boil, lower the heat, and simmer, partially covered, until the barley and beans are cooked, about 1 hour.

Meanwhile, warm the olive oil in a large skillet. Add the onions, celery, and mushrooms (including the porcinis). Cover and cook 10 minutes over medium-low heat, until the vegetables are softened. Uncover, raise the heat to medium, and cook 10 minutes, stirring from time to time until the mushrooms have browned and the bits stuck to the bottom of the pan are deep golden. Add the fennel and coriander and stir for a minute or so. Add the remaining 2 cups of stock and scrape up any bits that have stuck to the bottom of the pan.

Add the vegetables to the barley and beans along with the shoyu and sherry. Simmer for 20 minutes, partially covered, to finish cooking the soup and to marry the flavors. Stir in the dill, lemon juice, and a sprinkling of black pepper. Stir in the peas and let sit in the hot liquid for 3 to 4 minutes. Taste and add additional salt if necessary. Serve hot.

For best results, buy your barley in a natural foods store. Although you can use pearled, semipearled, and hull-less barley, I find the semipearled (known as hulled) to be my favorite for its chewy texture.

Make sure to wash the cremini mushrooms before using; they are full of grit.

Pierogis

The quintessential Eastern European comfort food, pierogis are essential for a Polish-style Christmas Eve. I fell in love with cabbage pierogis when I first sampled a glorious sauerkraut-filled version at my friend Alison Dearborne Rieder's home. Alison started making pierogis in her Polish grandmother's Vermont farmhouse when she was a little girl, and she makes them with her children every Christmas Eve.

Pierogi Dough

THIS RECIPE is compliments of my friend Dave's mother, Jean Anderson, a Ukrainian Canadian who makes pierogis for her family every year on Christmas Eve. The mashed potatoes make this dough especially tender.

MAKES 36 PIEROGIS

2 cups unbleached white flour
1 teaspoon salt
½ cup cold Dry Mashed Potatoes (page 83)
2 egg yolks
⅓ cup water
1 tablespoon extra virgin olive oil

Sauerkraut and Cabbage, Dilled Potato Cheese, or Swiss Chard filling
(pages 80–82)

Whisk the flour and salt together in a large bowl. Add the mashed potatoes and rub them into the flour with your hands, pressing out any large lumps.

Whisk together the yolks, water, and oil in a small bowl. Pour the liquid into the potato and flour mixture and mix, squeezing the dough together by hand. Turn the dough out onto a lightly floured board and knead just until smooth. (Too much kneading will toughen the dough.) Divide the dough into 2 balls. Rub a little oil over the balls and wrap in plastic. Let rest for at least 10 minutes.

Alternatively, use a food processor method: Pulse together the flour and salt. Add the potatoes and pulse a few times until evenly distributed. In a small bowl, whisk together the yolks, water, and oil. Pour the liquid into the food processor and process 15 to 30 seconds until the dough forms a ball. Divide into 2 balls, lightly oil, and wrap in plastic. Let rest for at least 10 minutes.

Have ready a baking sheet covered with parchment paper or a dusting of flour for the finished pierogis.

Roll the dough, one ball at a time, on a lightly floured surface until very thin. Cut out circles with a 3-inch cookie cutter or a glass. Place the circles on the baking sheet and cover with a damp towel to keep them from drying out. Roll out the scraps only one time; you should get 18 pierogis per ball of dough.

To fill, place a teaspoon of filling in the center of the dough. Fold over to form a half circle. Press to seal well (adding a dab of water on the edge to help seal if necessary), leaving a 1/4-inch border. Once you have rolled and filled the pierogis from the first ball of dough, re-cover the baking sheet with the damp towel and repeat the process with the second ball.

At this point you can freeze the pierogis on the baking sheet, then stack in freezer bags. Cook them without defrosting.

To cook, bring a large pot of water to a boil. Add the pierogis without crowding and cook until they float to the top, about 5 minutes. Serve hot.

Pierogi Fillings

The three fillings here include a sauerkraut-cabbage, a classic potato lightened with a bit of cheese and enhanced with chopped dill, and a chard with rosemary and lemon.

They are all easily made in advance and frozen, ready to be taken from the freezer to the pot. Serve them with Fresh Applesauce and Sautéed Onions (page 83).

Sauerkraut and cabbage

MAKES 2 CUPS (ENOUGH FOR 36 PIEROGIS)

2 tablespoons extra virgin olive oil
1 cup thinly sliced onion
Salt and freshly ground black pepper
2 cups shredded cabbage
1 ½ cups sauerkraut
2 tablespoons butter

Preheat the oven to 400°F.

Warm the olive oil in a large skillet. Add the onion and a sprinkling of salt and black pepper, and cook over medium heat for about 12 to 15 minutes, until the onion is softened and browned. Add the cabbage and cook another 10 minutes or so, just until the cabbage is wilted. Mix in the sauerkraut and adjust the seasonings.

Spread the cabbage mixture in an 8 x 8-inch baking pan. Cut the butter into pieces and distribute it over the cabbage. Cover with aluminum foil and bake 45 minutes to let the flavors marry. Remove from the oven and cool to room temperature before filling the pierogis.

Dilled Potato Cheese

MAKES 2 CUPS (ENOUGH FOR 36 PIEROGIS)

2 tablespoons butter

1 cup finely diced onion

1½ cups Dry Mashed Potatoes (page 83)

½ cup ricotta or farmer cheese

2 tablespoons chopped dill

½ teaspoon salt

Melt the butter in a medium skillet. Add the onion and sauté over medium-high heat until golden, about 8 minutes. Transfer to a bowl with the potatoes, cheese, dill, and salt and combine thoroughly. Taste and add additional salt if necessary.

Swiss Chard with Rosemary and Lemon

MAKES 2 CUPS (ENOUGH FOR 36 PIEROGIS)

2 bunches Swiss chard or spinach, stems removed, roughly chopped,
    and washed (1 ½ to 2 pounds)
3 tablespoons extra virgin olive oil
4 garlic cloves, minced
Salt and freshly ground black pepper
2 teaspoons minced fresh rosemary
1 cup farmer or ricotta cheese
Grated zest of 1 lemon
1 egg yolk

Cook the chard in a large pot or skillet over medium heat, stirring frequently or tossing with tongs to push the uncooked leaves to the bottom of the pot. You don't have to add water to the pot because the water clinging to the leaves from washing is enough to cook them. Cook until the leaves have wilted and are bright green.

Drain the chard and squeeze out any excess liquid. Chop finely.

Warm the oil with the garlic in a medium skillet over medium heat. When the garlic just begins to color, add the chard and stir to warm through. Season to taste with salt and black pepper. Remove from the heat and stir in the rosemary.

Place in a medium bowl and stir in the cheese and lemon zest. Taste and adjust the salt and pepper if necessary. Stir in the egg yolk.

Dry Mashed Potatoes

Cover 1½ pounds russet potatoes with water in a medium pot. Add 2 teaspoons salt and bring to a boil. Cook until tender, about 30 minutes. Drain and peel the potatoes. (You may need to hold the hot potatoes with an oven mitt or towel.) Mash and let them cool to room temperature.

MAKES 3 CUPS DRY MASHED POTATOES, ENOUGH TO USE
FOR THE POTATO FILLING AND 3 BATCHES OF PIEROGI DOUGH

Fresh Applesauce

Peel 4 apples (McIntosh are good for sauce) and quarter them. Cut each quarter into 3 pieces, then cut in half. Add them to a pot with 1 cup apple juice or cider, a sprinkling of nutmeg, and a sprinkling of salt. Bring to a boil, covered. Uncover and cook at a rapid simmer until the apples are completely tender and mushy, about 20 minutes. Smash the apples into sauce.

MAKES 2 CUPS FRESH APPLESAUCE

Sautéed Onions

Warm 2 tablespoons butter and 1 tablespoon extra virgin olive oil in a medium skillet. Add 2 cups finely diced onion and cook over medium heat, stirring every so often, until deeply golden, about 10 minutes.

MAKES ¾ CUP

Lemony Trout with Herbs and Bread Crumbs

HERBED TROUT fillets are baked under a layer of lemon slices, which infuse the fish with citrusy flavor. This festive dish takes only minutes to prepare.

SERVES 4 TO 6

8 rainbow trout fillets
Salt and freshly ground black pepper
4 tablespoons (½ stick) unsalted butter
2 teaspoons Dijon mustard
¼ cup chopped parsley
2 tablespoons chopped dill
24 thin lemon slices (from 2 to 3 lemons)
I tablespoon extra virgin olive oil
½ cup bread crumbs, preferably whole wheat

Preheat the oven to 450°F. Arrange the trout, skin side down, on a parchment-covered baking sheet. Sprinkle the fillets evenly with salt and black pepper.

Melt the butter in a small saucepan and stir in the mustard. Drizzle the mixture over the trout and sprinkle on the fresh herbs. Place the lemon slices along each trout, about 3 per trout. Roast until the fillets flake easily when pricked with a fork, about 10 minutes.

Meanwhile, warm the oil in a medium skillet over medium heat. Add the bread crumbs and stir until toasted, about 3 to 4 minutes. When the fish comes out of the oven, remove the lemon slices and sprinkle each fillet with the bread crumbs.

If your fish market only sells the trout whole, ask the fishmonger to cut them into fillets and remove the fins.

Gingery Beet Relish with Horseradish

THIS ZESTY relish provides a bright counterpoint to the rest of the menu.

MAKES 3 CUPS

2 pounds medium beets (or 1½ pounds large)
1 tablespoon minced fresh ginger
2 tablespoons prepared horseradish
½ cup chopped parsley
¾ teaspoon salt
¼ cup balsamic vinegar

Place the beets in a medium pot or saucepan and cover with water. Bring to a boil, lower the heat, and simmer until the beets are tender, about 45 minutes to an hour for the medium, up to 1½ hours for the large. Alternatively, place the beets in a pressure cooker and cook over high pressure about 15 minutes for the medium, 25 minutes for the large, until tender.

Remove the beets from the water and place under running water to cool. Slip off the skins and let cool a few minutes.

Grate the beets using the shredding blade of the food processor or the large holes of a box grater. You should have 3 cups shredded beets.

Transfer the beets to a medium bowl. Add the ginger, horseradish, parsley, salt, and vinegar and toss to combine.

Note: Some gourmet stores sell Cryovac-packed cooked baby beets in 1-pound packages. These work very well for the recipe. You can also process the beets until finely chopped for an alternative texture.

cauliflower Green Bean Salad with Pickles

BLANCHED CAULIFLOWER and green beans are anything but boring in this crunchy salad. Chopped bits of pickle, radish, scallion, and herbs make every bite a refreshing surprise.

SERVES 6

4 cups bite-size cauliflower florets, from 1 small cauliflower
¼ pound green beans, cut into 1-inch pieces (1 cup)
½ cup dill pickle, cut into small dice
8 radishes, thinly sliced into rounds (½ cup)
¼ cup thinly sliced scallions, white and green parts
¼ cup chopped parsley
1 teaspoon fresh thyme leaves
2 garlic cloves, minced
3 tablespoons apple cider vinegar
¼ cup extra virgin olive oil
½ teaspoon salt
Freshly ground black pepper

Blanch the cauliflower in a medium pot of lightly salted boiling water until fork-tender, about 4 minutes. Remove with a slotted spoon and refresh with cold water. Drain well and transfer to a medium bowl. Blanch the green beans until tender, about 4 minutes. Refresh, drain well, and add to the cauliflower.

Stir in the pickle, radishes, scallions, parsley, thyme, and garlic.

Whisk together the vinegar, oil, salt, and a sprinkling of black pepper in a small bowl. Stir into the vegetables to combine. Let sit for 20 minutes to let the flavors marry. Taste and stir in a sprinkling more salt and pepper if necessary. Serve at room temperature.

Cheese Blintzes with Crimson Compote

CHEESE BLINTZES are elevated from homey to elegant when draped in a brilliant apple-cranberry compote. The blintz batter, made with whole wheat pastry flour and yogurt, cooks up into paper-thin, delectable pancakes.

MAKES 10 TO 12 BLINTZES (SERVES 5 OR 6)

Blintz Batter

3 eggs

¾ cup plain yogurt

2 tablespoons water

2 tablespoons natural sugar, such as Sucanat, maple, or evaporated cane sugar

½ teaspoon salt

2 tablespoons butter, melted

¾ cup whole wheat pastry flour

Butter or coconut oil, to cook the blintzes

Filling

1½ cups farmer cheese

¼ cup natural sugar, such as maple or evaporated cane sugar

2 tablespoons plain yogurt

1 teaspoon grated lemon zest

1 teaspoon vanilla extract

Salt

2 egg yolks

2 tablespoons butter, melted, for baking

MAKE THE BLINTZ BATTER: In a stand blender, blend the eggs, yogurt, water, sugar, salt, butter, and flour together. Let the batter rest for 15 minutes.

Lightly grease a 10- to 12-inch nonstick skillet with melted butter or oil, using a paper

(continued)

towel. Warm the pan over medium-high heat. Pour about ¼ cup batter into the pan, tipping the pan in a circular motion so that batter covers the entire surface. Cook until the crêpe bubbles and becomes golden around the edges, about 45 seconds. Loosen the edges with a spatula, and then with the spatula or your hands, flip it over. Cook for about 5 to 10 seconds on the second side. Slide the finished crêpe onto a plate.

Continue to cook the crêpes over medium-high heat until the batter is finished. If at any time during the cooking process the batter feels like it has thickened, add a tablespoon or so of water to thin it out.

MAKE THE FILLING: In a medium bowl, mix together the cheese, sugar, yogurt, zest, vanilla, a pinch of salt, and the yolks.

Dollop a heaping tablespoon of filling along the bottom of a pancake. Fold the sides in a few inches and roll up the crêpe like a jelly roll. Repeat with the other pancakes.

Line them up in an 8 x 8-inch baking dish. Preheat the oven to 400°F.

Drizzle the melted butter over the blintzes and bake until browned, about 15 minutes.

Blintzes can be filled and then frozen without losing taste or texture. Do not thaw before cooking; pour the melted butter on the blintzes and bake for 25 minutes.

Crimson Compote

*T*HE COMPOTE keeps refrigerated for 2 weeks.

MAKES 3 CUPS

2 Golden Delicious apples
One 3-inch piece orange zest
One 3-inch piece lemon zest
1 cinnamon stick
½ cup currants
½ cup dried apricots, cut into ¼-inch dice
½ cup dried cherries
¾ cup fresh or frozen cranberries
1 cup Madeira or sherry
¼ cup maple syrup
1 cup water
1 vanilla bean

Peel and quarter the apples, cut out the cores, and cut each quarter into 3 wedges. Add the apples, zests, cinnamon stick, currants, apricots, cherries, cranberries, Madeira, and maple syrup to a medium saucepan along with the water.

Split the vanilla bean in half lengthwise and scrape out the tiny seeds with the tip of a knife. Add the beans and scraped pod to the liquid. Cover and bring to a boil. Lower the heat, remove the lid, and simmer rapidly, uncovered, until the compote has thickened and the apples and cranberries are cooked, about 15 minutes. Remove the zests, vanilla pods, and cinnamon stick. Transfer to a bowl and cool to room temperature. Refrigerate until cool. Serve spooned over the blintzes.

christmas Day

F YOU PREFER TO have your feast on Christmas afternoon, consider an Italian-inspired spread. Lunch in the Italian tradition is the most important of all the Christmas feasts and is a lengthy affair: the family sits around the table for hours talking or receiving guests and playing games. Presents may be exchanged on Christmas Day, but it is more traditional to wait until Epiphany. Children receive a stocking filled with sweets if they've been good or with "coal," made of black sugar, if they've misbehaved. It's not St. Nicholas who delivers the gifts, but a kind old crone, la Befana. It is said that she followed the wise men but lost her way and has been wandering ever since, handing out presents to children at Christmas.

This feast is ideal for entertaining: since you can make almost all of the dishes beforehand, there's no last-minute fussing. Sweet bell peppers, simmered with mushrooms, olives, and capers, are delicious piled onto toasted bread. A seasonal pumpkin portobello lasagna makes a celebratory crowd pleaser. The stuffed flounder fillets are filled with a pesto made from pistachios, bread crumbs, lemon, and mint and take just minutes to bake. The Ribollita Soup, a Tuscan-inspired specialty, is a hearty-tasting yet light soup. In the salad, peppery lettuces contrast with tart apples and sprinkles of robust blue cheese. Side dishes of braised cipollini onions with grapes and broccoli rabe with roasted cherry tomatoes are especially festive. Chocolate-filled nut sandwich cookies make great afternoon treats.

Cook's Notes

Up to several weeks in advance:

Make a stock for the soup.

3 days in advance:

Make the tomato sauce for the lasagna.

2 days in advance:

Make the peperonata.
Make the pistachio pesto.
Make the salad dressing.
Roast the squash and mushrooms for the lasagna.
Make the chocolate sandwich cookies.

Day before:

Assemble the lasagna and bake.
Make the Ribollita Soup.
Make the cipollini onions.
Blanch the broccoli rabe.

Day of:

Reheat the lasagna.
Bake the cherry tomatoes.
Sauté the broccoli rabe.
Roll up the flounder and bake.
Wash the salad greens, cut the apples, and assemble the salad.
Toast the bread for the peperonata.

Bruschetta with Peperonata

*H*ERE'S A zesty starter to whet your appetite. Sweet bell peppers braise with mushrooms, olives, and capers into a vibrant bruschetta topping. Toss leftovers onto pasta for a quick meal.

MAKES 3 CUPS

¼ cup extra virgin olive oil
4 bell peppers, preferably a mix of red, yellow, and/or orange, cut into ½-inch dice
½ pound cremini mushrooms, thinly sliced (4 cups)
I cup diced onion
3 garlic cloves, minced
¼ cup pitted kalamata olives, cut into rings
¼ cup pitted green olives, cut into rings
I tablespoon capers
½ cup chopped parsley
I tablespoon red wine vinegar
Salt and freshly ground black pepper

I baguette, cut into ½-inch diagonal slices
2 garlic cloves, peeled and left whole

Preheat the oven to 300°F.

Warm the olive oil in a large skillet. Add the bell peppers, mushrooms, and onion and cook over medium heat for 15 minutes, until the peppers are softened and the mushrooms have released a lot of liquid. Add the minced garlic, olives, and capers and cook an additional 5 minutes. Stir in the parsley, vinegar, ½ teaspoon salt, and a sprinkling of black pepper. Taste and add more salt if necessary.

Place the bread on a baking sheet and place in the oven. Heat until the bread is crisp, about 5 minutes. Turn and repeat with the other side until both sides are crisp. Remove from the oven and rub one side with the whole garlic. Serve topped with the peperonata.

Ribollita Soup

*T*USCANS HAVE a long history of ingenious uses for stale bread. In this classic, a couple of slices of bread add body to a rustic vegetable soup, which looks thick and hearty but is surprisingly light. Serve it over an additional piece of bread and drizzle it with your favorite extra virgin olive oil.

Buy a Tuscan or country bread and let the loaf sit out for a couple of days to get stale. The soup lasts for up to 5 days in the refrigerator. Although the soup is tasty without any stock at all, the roasted vegetable stock adds another layer of flavor.

SERVES 4 TO 6

¾ cup great Northern beans, soaked (see page 11)

7 cups water or vegetable stock (pages 4–6)

4 thyme sprigs

Salt and freshly ground black pepper

2 tablespoons extra virgin olive oil, plus more for drizzling

1 cup onion, cut into small dice

1 medium carrot, cut into small dice (½ cup)

1 celery stalk, cut into small dice (½ cup)

2 cups shredded cabbage (¼ head of a medium cabbage)

One 14-ounce can whole plum tomatoes, drained and coarsely chopped (about 7)

1 small, thin-skinned potato (¼ pound), cut into small dice (½ cup)

1 small zucchini (¼ pound), cut into small dice (¾ cup)

2 slices stale country bread, crusts removed, torn into pieces, plus 1 extra piece for
   each bowl

¼ cup chopped parsley, for garnish

Drain the beans. Place the beans, 4 cups water or stock, and the thyme in a medium pot. Cover and bring to a boil. Lower the heat and simmer until the beans are tender, about 1 hour. Stir in ¾ teaspoon salt and a sprinkling of black pepper. Remove and discard the thyme.

Meanwhile, warm the olive oil in a medium pot. Add the onion, carrot, celery, and

(continued)

cabbage and cook over medium heat for about 15 minutes, until the vegetables are soft-ened. Add the tomatoes, potato, zucchini, and 3 cups water or stock. Cover and bring to a boil. Lower the heat and simmer until the potato is softened, about 15 minutes.

Add the cooked beans along with the cooking liquid to the pot. Add additional water if necessary if the soup is too thick.

Stir in the 2 slices of torn bread and let simmer 5 minutes to thicken the soup and ab-sorb the flavors. Taste and adjust the salt if necessary.

To serve, place a piece of bread in each bowl. Ladle the hot soup over the bread. Drizzle each plate with olive oil and sprinkle with parsley.

Note: If your bread is fresh, cut into slices and place in a 200°F oven until it is stale.

Watercress and Endive Salad with Apple and Blue Cheese

*P*EPPERY LETTUCES pair with thinly sliced tart apple and robust cheese for a delightful taste sensation. Raw artisanal blue cheeses are readily available and have especially great flavor.

SERVES 6

2 bunches watercress, hard stems removed (½ pound)

2 heads endive, any discolored leaves removed and discarded (¾ pound),
    cut into ¼-inch-wide lengthwise spears

1 tablespoon fresh lemon juice

1 tablespoon sherry vinegar

¼ teaspoon Dijon mustard

1 teaspoon honey

6 tablespoons extra virgin olive oil

Salt and freshly ground black pepper

1 Granny Smith apple, peeled and cut into very thin strips (1 heaping cup)

6 tablespoons crumbled blue cheese (from a 3-ounce chunk)

Place the watercress and endive in a medium bowl. Whisk together the lemon juice and sherry vinegar in a small bowl with the mustard and honey. Drizzle in the olive oil and whisk to combine. Sprinkle with salt and black pepper to taste. Stir the apple strips into the lettuces. Toss with the dressing and divide onto plates, sprinkled with about 1 tablespoon crumbled blue cheese per serving.

Squash-Portobello Lasagna

ORTOBELLO MUSHROOMS, sweet squash, and tomatoes combine for a colorful and un-usual take on a favorite. Kabocha squash, with its dense flesh, makes this lasagna particu-larly special, but you can substitute butternut, the old standby. Prepare this ahead to make your Christmas entertaining effortless.

There's no need to cook the noodles. They cook in the sauce while the lasagna bakes. Make the sauce while the squash and mushrooms bake.

You'll have about 2 cups extra sauce to serve with the lasagna.

SERVES 8

MAKES 4 HEAPING CUPS OF TOMATO SAUCE

Squash

One 3-pound kabocha squash

1 tablespoon extra virgin olive oil

1 cup onion, cut into small dice

1 teaspoon salt

Freshly ground black pepper

2 tablespoons chopped fresh sage

Mushrooms

1½ pounds portobello mushrooms

¼ cup extra virgin olive oil

¾ teaspoon salt

Freshly ground black pepper

10 fresh thyme sprigs

Tomato Sauce

¼ cup extra virgin olive oil

4 garlic cloves, minced

¼ teaspoon red pepper flakes

2 fresh rosemary sprigs

Two 28-ounce cans crushed tomatoes, preferably fire-roasted

I teaspoon salt

Freshly ground black pepper

2 teaspoons sugar

I teaspoon balsamic vinegar

½ cup chopped fresh basil

½ pound lasagna noodles (about 12)

1½ pounds ricotta cheese, preferably fresh

I pound fresh mozzarella, thinly sliced

I cup grated Parmesan cheese

ROAST THE SQUASH: Preheat the oven to 375°F. Place the whole squash in the oven for 15 minutes to soften. Remove from the oven and cut it in half. Roast it, cut side down, until tender, about 40 minutes. Let cool enough to handle. Remove and discard the seeds and scoop out the flesh. You should have about 3 cups.

Warm the oil in a medium skillet. Add the onion and sauté over medium heat until golden, about 10 minutes. Stir in the squash, salt, and a sprinkling of black pepper. Cook for 5 minutes or so to evaporate the liquid from the squash. Stir in the sage. Taste and add more salt if necessary.

ROAST THE MUSHROOMS: Remove the stems and wipe the mushroom caps clean. Cut the caps into ½-inch slices. Toss the mushrooms in a bowl with the oil, salt, and a sprinkling of black pepper. Place on a parchment-covered baking sheet and lay the thyme sprigs over the mushrooms. Roast for 40 minutes, tossing a couple of times, until the mushrooms are shriveled and intensely flavored. Remove from the oven and discard the thyme sprigs.

MAKE THE SAUCE: Warm the oil, garlic, red pepper flakes, and rosemary sprigs in a medium pot over medium heat. When the garlic is straw colored, after 3 minutes, add the tomatoes and salt. Bring to a boil, lower the heat, and simmer, partially covered, about 40 minutes. Stir in a sprinkling of black pepper, the sugar, balsamic vinegar, and basil. Discard the rosemary. Taste and add more salt if necessary.

Reserve 2 cups of sauce to serve with the lasagna.

(continued)

MAKE THE LASAGNA: Preheat the oven to 350°F. Use an 8 x 11-inch baking pan and layer the ingredients as follows: one-third of the sauce, a layer of noodles, half the ricotta cheese topped with a thin layer (one-third) of mozzarella, 1 cup of the squash and all of the mushrooms, another layer of noodles, another third of the sauce, the remaining ricotta and a thin layer (one-third) of mozzarella, the remaining squash, another layer of noodles, the last third of the sauce, and the rest of the mozzarella and all of the Parmesan.

Place the lasagna in the oven on a baking sheet and bake, uncovered, for about 20 minutes, until the top is just beginning to brown. Tent the pan with foil, being as careful as possible not to disturb the cheese, and bake an additional 40 minutes, until the pasta is cooked through and the juices are bubbling. Remove the tent and let cook an additional 10 minutes or so, uncovered, to brown the top. Remove from the oven and let rest for at least 10 minutes before cutting. Serve hot.

Flounder Roll-ups with Pistachio Pesto

A FRESH BLEND of pistachios, lemon, mint, and bread crumbs combine into an unusual pesto. If the fillets are on the larger side, cut them in half after baking. You can make the pesto days in advance; the fish takes only minutes to prepare.

SERVES 6

½ cup fresh bread crumbs
½ cup shelled pistachios
2 garlic cloves, peeled
Grated zest of 1 lemon
1 tablespoon fresh lemon juice
2 tablespoons fresh mint leaves
Salt and freshly ground black pepper
¼ cup extra virgin olive oil
2 pounds flounder fillets (5 or 6 pieces)

Preheat the oven to 400°F.

MAKE THE PESTO: In the bowl of a food processor fitted with the steel blade, place the bread crumbs, pistachios, garlic, lemon zest, lemon juice, mint, ½ teaspoon salt, and a sprinkling of black pepper. Process until coarsely chopped, scraping down the sides as necessary. Add the olive oil and pulse a couple of times to combine. The pesto should be chunky.

On a parchment-covered baking sheet, arrange the fillets so that the more attractive side is face down. Sprinkle the exposed side with salt and pepper. Spread a heaping tablespoon of pesto along the length of each whole piece of fish. Roll up the fish starting at the narrow end and place, seam side down, on the prepared sheet.

Sprinkle the remaining pesto over the top of the fish. Bake for 10 to 15 minutes, until cooked through. Remove from the oven and slice each roll in half crosswise. Serve hot.

Roasted Cherry Tomatoes with Sautéed Broccoli Rabe

BROCCOLI RABE and roasted cherry tomatoes make an exciting vegetable dish in the colors of Christmas. Your kitchen will smell heavenly as the tomatoes roast with rosemary and garlic.

A quick dip in a pot of boiling salted water takes the bitter edge off of the broccoli rabe. For a change, pair the tomatoes with other vegetables, such as spinach.

SERVES 4

Roasted Tomatoes

1 pint cherry tomatoes

3 tablespoons extra virgin olive oil

1 tablespoon balsamic vinegar

Salt and freshly ground black pepper

3 garlic cloves, thinly sliced

4 fresh rosemary sprigs

Broccoli Rabe

2 bunches broccoli rabe (1 ½ pounds)

4 whole garlic cloves

2 tablespoons extra virgin olive oil

Salt and freshly ground black pepper

Preheat the oven to 375°F.

Spread the tomatoes on a small baking dish (8 x 8-inch Pyrex is ideal).

Drizzle the tomatoes with the olive oil, vinegar, $\frac{1}{2}$ teaspoon salt, a sprinkling of black pepper, and the sliced garlic. Tuck the rosemary among the tomatoes. Roast, uncovered, 30 minutes, until the tomatoes are shriveled and juicy. Discard the rosemary.

Meanwhile, cut off the hard stems of the broccoli rabe. Blanch the greens in a large pot of boiling salted water until bright green, about 3 to 4 minutes. Remove to a bowl filled with cold or ice water to stop the cooking.

Drain the greens and cut them into bite-size pieces.

Smash the whole garlic cloves. Warm the oil with the garlic in a large skillet over medium heat until the garlic is lightly golden, about 2 to 3 minutes. Immediately add the greens and stir to heat through and combine. Sprinkle with salt and black pepper. Gently stir in the tomatoes. Serve immediately.

Cipollini in Agrodolce

THESE ELEGANT oval onions are caramelized, then braised with wine and vinegar. Grapes lend a sweet juiciness.

SERVES 4

1 tablespoon extra virgin olive oil
1 tablespoon butter
1 ½ pounds cipollini onions, peeled and left whole (see Note)
¼ cup white wine
2 tablespoons sugar, preferably natural sugar
2 tablespoons balsamic vinegar
1 bay leaf
Salt and freshly ground black pepper
½ cup seedless red grapes, halved
¼ cup fresh parsley leaves (optional)

Heat the oil and butter over medium-high heat in a large skillet. Add the onions and sauté until golden on both sides, about 3 minutes per side.

Add the wine, sugar, vinegar, bay leaf, and a sprinkling of salt and black pepper. Bring to a boil and cover. Lower the heat and simmer for 20 minutes.

Uncover, add the grapes, and stir to warm them through, about 5 minutes. Remove the bay leaf. Transfer the onions to a dish and garnish with parsley if desired. Serve hot or at room temperature.

Note: To peel the onions whole, cut a thin slice off the root and stem ends of the onion. Make a slit in the skin and peel off the outer layer.

Chocolate Hazelnut Sandwich Cookies

THESE MELT-IN-YOUR-MOUTH cookies are fun to nibble after a Christmas Day feast. Browning the butter until nutty and fragrant makes all the difference. You can vary the flavor of the cookies by choosing different sugars.

MAKES 26 COOKIES

1 stick unsalted butter
¾ cup sugar, such as evaporated cane sugar or maple sugar
2 teaspoons vanilla extract
1 egg, lightly beaten
1 cup hazelnuts, skins removed
1 cup whole wheat pastry flour
⅛ teaspoon salt
1 teaspoon baking soda
4 ounces semisweet chocolate

Melt the butter in a small saucepan over medium heat and cook, stirring occasionally, until the butter turns golden with a nutlike fragrance and flecks on the bottom of the pan turn a rich caramel brown, about 5 minutes. The butter will foam at first, then stop, and then a thicker foam will cover the surface just before the butter begins to brown.

When the butter is browned and nutty, immediately pour it into a medium bowl, add the sugar and vanilla, and whisk to combine. Let cool a few minutes, then stir in the egg.

Grind the hazelnuts in a food processor until floury. Transfer the ground hazelnuts to another medium bowl. Whisk them together with the flour, salt, and baking soda. Scrape the butter mixture into the dry ingredients, stirring together just until the dry ingredients are thoroughly moistened. Cover and place in the refrigerator for at least 1 hour to firm.

Preheat the oven to 325°F. Position a rack in the middle of the oven.

Pull off a piece of dough about the size of an egg. Roll it into a log about ¾ inch in diameter. Cut the log into 1-inch pieces and roll these into balls. Place on a baking sheet 2 inches apart and flatten slightly. Continue with the rest of the dough. Bake 10 minutes, turning the baking sheet once, until the undersides are lightly golden. Remove from the oven and transfer the baking sheet to a rack and cool completely, about 20 minutes.

Melt the chocolate in a double boiler. Dollop some chocolate on the flat side of one cookie and sandwich with the flat side of another cookie. Continue with the remaining cookies, then let stand until set, about 30 minutes. Transfer the cookies to an airtight container.

Note: The dough can be made up to a day in advance. Bring to room temperature to soften slightly before forming the cookies.

Cookies keep in an airtight container at room temperature for 2 weeks.

Kwanzaa

KWANZAA IS A UNIQUE seven-day celebration that reaffirms the ancestry and culture of the African-American community. Founded in 1966 by Dr. Maulana Karenga in the midst of the black freedom movement, the holiday is rooted in harvest celebrations practiced in various African cultures. Kwanzaa has since grown from a mostly African-American holiday to one celebrated by millions of Africans throughout the world African community.

The name comes from the Swahili word *kwanza* (with one *a*), meaning "first," as in the phrase *matunda ya kwanza*, which means "first fruits."

The seven guiding principles of family and community, self-determination, collective work and responsibility, cooperative economy, purpose, creativity, and faith are of the utmost importance. Though Kwanzaa is celebrated at the end of the year, from December 26 through January 1, it is neither a religious holiday nor a replacement for the other year-end holidays such as Christmas and New Year's. It may be celebrated jointly with any or all of them. The healing supper usually takes place on the sixth day, to reaffirm a commitment to the betterment of life for all African-Americans.

This Ethiopian menu makes a great Kwanzaa celebration. Traditional dining in Ethiopia is characterized by sharing food from a common plate, a practice that signifies loyalty, family, and friendship bonds. There is an Ethiopian expression that has resonance for the contemporary Pan-African community: "It is said that people who eat from the same plate will never betray one another."

Whether or not you choose to eat communally or fill your own plate with injera and the various we'ts (spicy stews with Berbere) and alichas (mild stews), here are all the important components of an Ethiopian feast. It's a great meal for a gathering, since virtually the entire meal can be prepared in advance and reheated. Prepare the Berbere, the essential red paste made up of a combination of herbs, spices, and chiles, and Nit'ir Qibe, the clarified butter flavored with onions, garlic, ginger, and spices, and the rest of the feast comes together quickly. The pleasantly spongy Injera Teff Crêpe is a quick version that doesn't require a long fermentation. Though the lentil stew, squash, chicken, and collards have either the spiced clarified butter or the Berbere paste in their ingredients, they all have distinct flavors.

These dishes are complemented by the chunky and milder Ethiopian vegetables and the red lentils, as well as the refreshing Red Onion, Tomato, and Mint Salad. With their different textures and colors, the dishes look beautiful on the plate. Serve the meal with a dollop of plain yogurt for cooling contrast. A light chocolate truffle, wonderful for a Valentine's Day celebration as well, lends just the right light, sweet finish.

Cook's Notes

Up to 3 weeks ahead:

Make the Berbere paste.
Make the Nit'ir Qibe.

2 days before:

Make the Chocolate Truffles.

Day before:

Make the Yemiser We't.
Make the Red Lentils with Peppers.
Make the Doro We't.
Make the Collards with Nit'ir Qibe.
Make the Amhari-Atklit.
Make the Squash with Berbere.

Day of:

Make the Quick Injera.
Make the Red Onion, Tomato, and Mint Salad.

Berbere (Ethiopian Chile and Spice Paste)

*T*RADITIONALLY MADE in huge quantities, berbere is the vibrant spice paste used in many Ethiopian dishes. This modest amount makes just enough to make all the Ethiopian recipes here, but it scales up well. You can also buy berbere powder from a well-stocked spice store (see Resources, page 251), but this vibrant paste comes together quickly and will keep for months.

MAKES 1 CUP PASTE

2 ounces dried New Mexican or pasilla chiles (2 loosely packed cups)
5 hot dried red chiles, such as Indian red chiles, Thai chiles, or chiles de arbol
1 tablespoon minced fresh ginger
2 tablespoons minced garlic
1/4 cup chopped red onion
1/2 cup water
Seeds from 2 green cardamom pods (see Note)
1/4 teaspoon fenugreek seed (see page 17)
1/2 teaspoon black peppercorns
1/4 teaspoon coriander seed
5 whole cloves
1/8 teaspoon ground cinnamon
1 teaspoon salt
1 cup finely chopped basil leaves

Cut the stems off the chiles. Open them and remove the seeds. (If you miss a few, it's not the end of the world.) Place the chiles in a medium pot with water to cover. Bring to a boil, turn off the heat, and let the chiles rest until softened, about 10 minutes.

Meanwhile, combine the ginger, garlic, onion, and water in a small saucepan and bring to a boil. Cook, uncovered, until the water is evaporated, about 5 minutes. Set aside. Dry-toast the cardamom seeds, fenugreek, peppercorns, coriander, and cloves together in a heavy skillet over medium-high heat until fragrant, stirring constantly, 2 to 3 minutes. Place in a mortar or spice grinder and grind to a powder.

Drain the chiles, discarding the soaking water. Place in a food processor along with the ginger-garlic mixture and the dried spices, including the cinnamon and salt. Process until you have a paste, scraping down the sides as necessary. Add the basil and process until well blended.

Spoon the paste into a clean glass jar. Seal well and refrigerate for up to 3 months.

Note: Crush the cardamom pods by pressing down with the side of a knife.

Nít'ír Qíbe (Spíced Clarífíed Butter)

*H*ERBS AND spices are cooked in the clarifying butter, then strained out, resulting in a fragrant and healthful cooking fat. Refrigerated, it keeps for 4 months. Make this along with the Berbere spice paste, so you can whip up any of the recipes in a flash.

MAKES 1 ½ CUPS

1 pound unsalted butter, preferably organic
¼ cup chopped red onion
3 garlic cloves, minced
One 1-inch piece unpeeled fresh ginger, grated
¼ teaspoon fenugreek seed (see page 17)
½ teaspoon turmeric
6 cardamom pods, crushed, pods and seeds (see Note above)
1 cinnamon stick
1 tablespoon roughly chopped fresh basil leaves

Melt the butter slowly in a small saucepan over medium-low heat until it is melted completely, about 5 minutes. The butter will start to gurgle as the water evaporates. When the top is covered with foam, add the other ingredients and reduce the heat to a simmer. Simmer gently on low heat, uncovered, until the milk solids start to brown on the bottom of the pot, about 10 to 15 minutes. After 10 minutes, check frequently, pushing aside any foam and tilting the pan to see if the solids have lightly browned. As soon as the solids turn light brown, turn off the heat and let the residue settle to the bottom. Pour the liquid through a double layer of cheesecloth into a heat-resistant container. Discard the solids.

Ni'tir Qibe keeps, covered and refrigerated, for up to 2 months.

Yemiser We't (Ethiopian Lentil Stew)

*T*HIS THICK lentil dish, highly flavored from the spiced clarified butter and Berbere, is a wonderful part of any Ethiopian gathering.

SERVES 6

¼ cup Nit'ir Qibe (page 111)
2 cups finely chopped onion
3 garlic cloves, minced or pressed
1 tablespoon Berbere (page 110)
2 teaspoons ground cumin
2 teaspoons paprika
1½ cups dried brown lentils
4 cups water
Salt
1 teaspoon fresh lemon juice
Freshly ground black pepper
Plain yogurt (optional)

Warm the Nit'ir Qibe in a medium saucepan. Add the onion and garlic and sauté over medium heat for about 7 minutes, or until the onion is just translucent. Add the Berbere, cumin, and paprika, and sauté for a few minutes more, stirring occasionally to prevent burning. Mix in the lentils with the water and 1¼ teaspoons salt. Cover and bring to a boil. Lower the heat and cook about an hour or so, partially covered, until the lentils are quite tender. Check now and then to see if there's enough liquid covering the lentils and add more water if necessary.

Stir in the lemon juice and add a sprinkling of black pepper. Taste and add more salt if necessary. Serve hot, with a dollop of yogurt if desired.

Red Lentils with Peppers

*T*HIS IS one of the mild dishes that doesn't use the spice paste or spiced clarified butter. The red lentils melt into a creamy mass in under 30 minutes.

SERVES 6

2 tablespoons extra virgin olive oil
2 cups onion, cut into small dice
3 garlic cloves, minced
1 tablespoon peeled minced fresh ginger
2 jalapeño peppers, preferably red, stemmed, seeded, and minced
1 teaspoon paprika
2 tablespoons tomato paste
2 cups red lentils, sorted and washed
4 cups water
Salt and freshly ground black pepper
1 teaspoon lemon juice

Warm the oil in a medium saucepan. Add the onion, garlic, ginger, and jalapeños and sauté over medium-low heat for about 10 minutes, until the onion is softened. Add the paprika and tomato paste and stir to combine.

Add the lentils and water, cover, and bring to a boil. Stir in 1 $3/4$ teaspoons salt, lower the heat, and cook, partially covered, for 20 minutes, until the lentils have melted down. Stir the lentils frequently to prevent sticking. Sprinkle with black pepper and stir in the lemon juice. Taste and adjust the salt if necessary.

Doro We't (Ethiopian Chicken Stew)

PROBABLY THE best-known Ethiopian dish, this version has skinless chicken cooked in a rich gravy until meltingly tender. It's a snap to make when you have the spiced clarified butter and Berbere already prepared.

SERVES 4 TO 6

1 whole chicken, cut up, skin removed and fat trimmed
Juice of 1 lime
1/4 cup Nit'ir Qibe (page 111)
2 cups chopped red onion
2 garlic cloves, minced
1/2 teaspoon ground ginger
6 tablespoons Berbere (page 110)
1 cup water
1/2 cup red wine
1 teaspoon salt

Soak the chicken in the lime juice with water to cover for 10 minutes. Drain the chicken. Warm the Nit'ir Qibe in a large skillet with sides. Add the red onion and garlic and cook over medium-low heat for about 10 minutes, until the onion is browned. Add the ginger, Berbere, water, wine, and salt and stir to combine. Add the chicken, turn to coat, and cover. Cook over medium heat until the chicken is tender, 30 to 40 minutes, flipping the chicken from time to time. Remove the chicken to a bowl as the pieces become fork-tender.

Uncover the pan and simmer rapidly to reduce the liquid to a sauce consistency, about 15 minutes. Return the chicken to the pan, along with any accumulated juices, and toss to coat in the sauce. Serve hot.

Buy a whole chicken and have the butcher cut it up for you. Cut each breast piece in half, so that you have 2 legs, 2 thighs, and 4 breast pieces. Remove the wing tips and save for stock along with the back. When you are skinning the chicken, trim off any fat. Don't try to remove the skin on the wings for this dish!

This dish is traditionally served with boiled eggs, which I've omitted here.

collards with Nit'ir Qibe

*I*N THIS tender braise, the collards cook slowly until they are mellow and delicious.

2 tablespoons Nit'ir Qibe (page 111)
1 medium onion, cut into small dice (1 cup)
2 garlic cloves, minced
1/4 teaspoon ground cardamom
1 pound collards, stemmed, chopped small
1 cup water
1/2 teaspoon salt
Freshly ground black pepper

Warm the Nit'ir Qibe in a large pot. Add the onion, garlic, and cardamom and sauté over medium heat for about 5 minutes, until the onion is softened. Add the collards, water, and salt and cover. Cook about 25 minutes, until the collards are very tender. Remove the lid and simmer, uncovered, about 5 minutes, until most of the liquid is evaporated. Sprinkle with black pepper and serve hot.

collard Greens

Of the commonly used hearty greens, collards are the most versatile and the mildest in taste. Collards have large, broad leaves and a stem that needs to be removed. Like kale, collards usually need to be cooked for at least 10 minutes, depending on how tough the leaves are, so a method like braising is a good choice. They don't lose that many nutrients from a longer cooking time, and the flavors benefit dramatically.

Squash with Berbere

BRIGHT ORANGE squash melds with rich Ethiopian flavors and cooks down into a thick purée. My first choice for this is kabocha, or any squash in the buttercup family, such as Red Kuri or Hokkaido pumpkin, but butternut squash will do.

SERVES 6

One 2½- to 3-pound winter squash such as kabocha, Hokkaido, or Red Kuri
3 tablespoons Nit'ir Qibe (page 111)
1 medium red onion, finely chopped (1 cup)
1 tablespoon Berbere (page 110)
2 cups water
¼ cup tomato paste
Salt
1 tablespoon maple syrup (optional)

Preheat the oven to 350°F. Place the whole squash on a baking sheet and bake for 30 minutes. Remove and let cool until you can handle the squash. Peel (the oven time will make peeling the squash easy and cut down on the cooking time) and seed the squash and cut it into 1-inch chunks. You should have about 6 cups.

Warm the Nit'ir Qibe in a medium saucepan. Add the onion and sauté for 7 to 10 minutes over medium-low heat until translucent. Add the Berbere and squash and stir to combine. Add 1 cup of water to the squash. Dissolve the tomato paste in the other cup of water in a small bowl. Add to the squash along with ½ teaspoon salt.

Cover and bring to a boil. Lower the heat to a rapid simmer and cook, covered, stirring from time to time, 10 minutes or so. Uncover and simmer until the squash is very tender, another 15 to 20 minutes, stirring from time to time. The squash will break apart and form a thick purée. As the purée gets thicker, stir more frequently. Add a little water if necessary if the squash is getting thick but is not yet ready. Taste and add the maple syrup if desired and a sprinkling more salt if necessary. Serve hot.

Amhari-Atklit (Vegetable Stew)

THIS MILD chunky vegetable stew, known as an *alicha,* contrasts beautifully with the rest of the dishes on the menu.

SERVES 6

2 tablespoons extra virgin olive oil

2 cups onion, cut into large dice

2 large carrots, peeled and cut into ½-inch diagonals (2 cups)

½ pound thin-skinned potatoes, peeled and cut into ¾-inch chunks (2 cups)

¼ head of a medium cabbage, cut into 1-inch cubes (2 cups)

1 tablespoon minced fresh ginger

½ teaspoon turmeric

1 teaspoon mustard seed

2 tablespoons tomato paste

1 cup water

1 teaspoon salt

½ pound green beans, trimmed and cut into 1-inch pieces (2 cups)

Warm the oil in a large pot. Add the onion, carrots, potatoes, and cabbage and cook over medium-low heat about 8 minutes, until the onion is softened. Add the ginger, turmeric, mustard seed, and tomato paste and stir to combine. Add the water and salt and cover. Cook until the vegetables start to soften, about 10 minutes. Add the green beans and cook until the vegetables are tender, an additional 15 minutes or so. Taste and adjust the salt if necessary.

Quick Injera (Teff Flour Crêpes)

HERE'S A speedy alternative to the Ethiopian bread, injera, made with teff, the smallest grain in the world. Club soda and baking soda keep this high-protein crêpe pleasantly spongy. For the best texture, make the crêpes immediately after mixing the batter. Cover the pan to cook the crêpes: There's no need to flip them.

MAKES 8 OR 9 PANCAKES

I cup teff flour (see Note)

¼ teaspoon baking soda

¼ teaspoon salt

2 tablespoons melted Nit'ir Qibe (page 111), melted butter, or melted coconut oil, plus oil for the pan

I tablespoon apple cider vinegar

I egg

1½ cups club soda

Place the teff flour, baking soda, salt, Nit'ir Qibe, vinegar, egg, and club soda in a blender and blend until smooth.

Lightly oil or butter a 10-inch nonstick skillet using a paper towel. Warm the pan over medium heat. Pour ¼ cup of batter into the pan, tipping the pan in a circular motion so that the batter covers the entire surface. Cover the pan and cook until the batter is no longer wet, tiny bubbles have formed on the surface, and the sides start to lift away from the pan, about 30 seconds to 1 minute. Slide or lift with a spatula from the pan onto a plate and cover. Repeat with the rest of the crêpes. You don't have to oil the pan in between pancakes. Stack the finished crêpes, keeping them covered. You can serve them at room temperature or warm them in an oven at 350°F.

You can also freeze these between layers of parchment with the entire stack covered in foil. Defrost and warm the whole packet in a 350°F oven for 15 minutes, until heated through.

Note: Teff is available in natural foods stores or through Bobsredmill.com.

Red Onion, Tomato, and Mint Salad

CHERRY TOMATOES, red onion, and mint are tossed together for a refreshing salad. Although not technically Ethiopian, the flavors complement the cooked dishes beautifully.

SERVES 6

1 cup red onion, thinly sliced into halved rings
3 cups cherry tomatoes, halved
1/4 cup chopped fresh mint leaves
Salt and freshly ground black pepper
2 tablespoons extra virgin olive oil
1 tablespoon red wine vinegar
1 tablespoon lemon juice

Soak the red onion in cold water for at least 15 minutes to take off the harsh edge. Drain and pat dry.

In a medium bowl, mix together gently the onion, tomatoes, mint leaves, and a generous sprinkling of salt and black pepper. Drizzle the salad with the oil and then stir in the vinegar and lemon juice. Toss gently to combine. Let the salad sit for 20 minutes to let the flavors marry.

chocolate Truffles

A MELT-IN-YOUR-MOUTH BITE of chocolate is the perfect ending to this Kwanzaa feast. The Spiced Clarified Butter lends a most delicious complexity to these truffles, but butter or coconut oil may be used instead. The key to their lightness is whipping the mixture until fluffy. These can be made a couple of days in advance and stored at room temperature.

MAKES 45 TRUFFLES

½ cup coconut milk or heavy cream
½ pound semisweet chocolate, chopped
2 tablespoons Nit'ir Qibe (page 111), butter, or coconut oil
2 tablespoons brandy or other liquor
⅓ cup cocoa powder

Heat the coconut milk or cream in a small pot until it just comes to a boil. Add the chocolate and let the mixture sit for 5 minutes, covered. Whisk to combine, then stir in the Nit'ir Qibe and brandy. Pour into a shallow container and refrigerate until semifirm, about 1 hour.

Scrape the mixture into a bowl and, using the paddle of a stand mixer, whip until fluffy. Use 2 teaspoons to drop scant teaspoons of chocolate onto a parchment-covered baking sheet. Refrigerate until the chocolate is firm, another 10 minutes or so.

Measure the cocoa powder into a bowl or shallow baking dish. Roll the truffles into balls and drop them into the cocoa to coat. Lift them out, shaking them off to remove any excess cocoa.

New Year's Eve

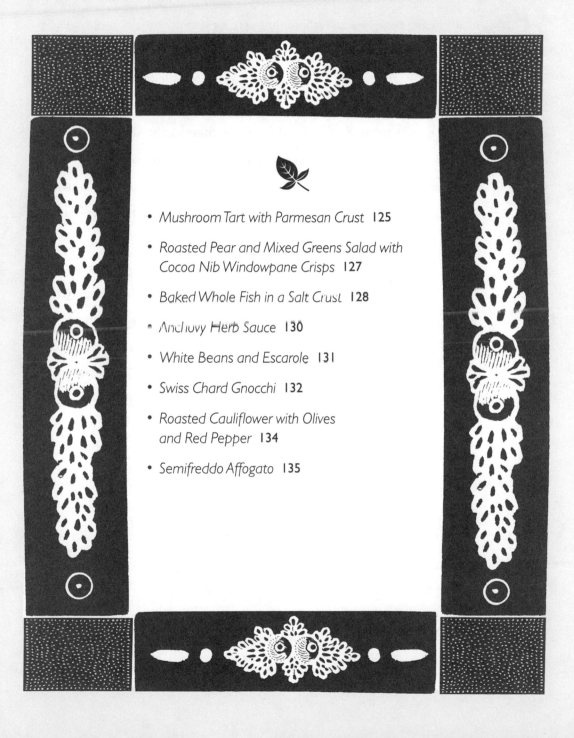

- *Mushroom Tart with Parmesan Crust* 125

- *Roasted Pear and Mixed Greens Salad with Cocoa Nib Windowpane Crisps* 127

- *Baked Whole Fish in a Salt Crust* 128

- *Anchovy Herb Sauce* 130

- *White Beans and Escarole* 131

- *Swiss Chard Gnocchi* 132

- *Roasted Cauliflower with Olives and Red Pepper* 134

- *Semifreddo Affogato* 135

THE EXCITEMENT IS PALPABLE as the last few minutes of December 31 tick by. "Auld Lang Syne," meaning "old long ago" or simply the "good old days," is played for countless gatherings around America as the ball drops in Times Square and the Miami Beach fireworks display reaches its finale. Celebrations on January 1 have civic origin rather than an astronomical or agricultural significance. Early Romans observed the New Year in late March, but in 153 B.C. the Romans changed the date to January 1 because it was the day after elections on which the new senators took office. In 45 B.C., Julius Caesar replaced the Egyptian solar calendar with the Julian calendar, with January 1 remaining New Year's Day. Although the date has long been set, the holiday as we know it in the West developed only in the last four hundred years.

Today, parties on New Year's Eve often last late into the night. Some common American traditions on New Year's Eve include champagne toasts and making loud noises, which comes out of a long tradition of chasing away evil spirits, and of course kissing at midnight. Personal traditions are diverse. There are as many ways to usher in the New Year as there are colors on a paint chart. While some people like to have large cocktail parties, others enjoy intimate soirées; some like to curl up with their sweethearts with some nibbles and a bottle of champagne in front of the fireplace.

The following morning, people make resolutions for the coming year. This tradition dates back to the early Babylonians, whose most popular resolution was to return borrowed farm equipment. Many of the superstitions associated with the event bear the common theme that activities engaged in on that day set the pattern for the year to come.

My personal favorite way of ushering in the New Year is the Italian way, with an intimate yet festive late night dinner, but should you wish to have a larger cocktail party, there are quite a few suitable recipes that can be pulled from the various starters in this book. The Mediterranean menu presented here matches the charged atmosphere of the evening, with unfussy but exciting fare. A luscious mushroom tart features balsamic syrup and a

Parmesan crust. A roasted pear and mixed greens salad has cocoa nib windowpane crisps spread throughout. The main course, although easy to put together, makes for high drama as you pull the whole salt-wrapped fish out of the oven and break open the crust. The fish is wrapped in a layer of grape leaves and is served with an anchovy herb sauce. There's a comforting dish of chard gnocchi floating in a rich bowl of white beans and escarole. The dessert, an almond Semifreddo Affogato, makes a grand finale, and can be made weeks in advance. Affogato means "drowned" in Italian, and this frozen dessert is doused with a splash of hot espresso poured over it right before serving. It's a wonderful interplay of cold and hot, bitter and sweet, with crunchy bits of candied almonds throughout, guaranteed to keep your guests lively well into the night. Make a toast and start your new year with joy and anticipation.

Cook's Notes

Week in advance:

Make the roasted vegetable or chicken stock (pages 4 and 5).
Make the crisps for the salad.
Make the pecan praline for the semifreddo.
Make the semifreddo.

2 days before:

Make the salad dressing.
Cook the white beans.

Day before:

Make the gnocchi and toss with oil (you can also make them further ahead and freeze).
Prepare the tart crust.
Make the salsa verde.

Day of:

Roast the cauliflower. Transfer to a baking dish and keep at room temperature.

Roast the pears for the salad.

Wrap the fish in the salt crust and refrigerate.

Prepare the lettuce.

Make the mushroom filling. Roll out the tart dough, fill, and bake.

Add the escarole to the white beans.

Right before dinner:

Bake the fish.

After dinner:

Make the coffee for the dessert.

Mushroom Tart with Parmesan Crust

THIS IS a truly luscious party dish. Caramelized onions and mushrooms combined with balsamic syrup are baked in a flaky Parmesan crust to make a rich yet delicate starter. Enjoy the tart warm from the oven or at room temperature.

If you have a wonderful bottle of great balsamic vinegar that is thick as syrup, available in gourmet markets or specialty stores such as Williams-Sonoma, use 2 tablespoons. If not, start with ¹/₂ cup balsamic vinegar and reduce to a syrup.

MAKES ONE 9-INCH TART
SERVES 6

Crust
¹/₂ cup unbleached white flour
¹/₄ cup whole wheat pastry flour
¹/₄ teaspoon salt
4 tablespoons (¹/₂ stick) unsalted butter, chilled and cut into small pieces
¹/₄ cup grated Parmesan cheese
2 tablespoons very cold water

Filling
¹/₄ cup extra virgin olive oil
2 cups thinly sliced onion
4 fresh thyme sprigs
¹/₂ pound cremini mushrooms, cleaned and quartered
¹/₂ pound portobello mushrooms, stems removed, caps cleaned and cut into 1-inch
    pieces
2 tablespoons balsamic syrup (or ¹/₂ cup balsamic vinegar)
1 egg, lightly beaten
¹/₂ cup grated Parmesan cheese
Salt and freshly ground black pepper

(continued)

MAKE THE CRUST: Place the flours and salt into the bowl of a food processor with the blade attached. Process for a couple of seconds to combine. Add the butter and pulse until the flour and butter become crumbs, about 7 to 10 pulses. The crumbs should be uneven, with some fine crumbs and some the size of small pebbles. Add the Parmesan and pulse to combine.

Add the water and pulse for a couple of seconds just to combine. Do not process until the dough becomes a ball.

Remove the dough from the bowl and gather into a ball. With the heel of your hand, push the dough forward onto a board to spread the butter and bind together. Form into a 4-inch flattened disk. Wrap in plastic and chill in the refrigerator for at least 1 hour before rolling out. You can keep the dough refrigerated for up to 3 days or frozen for up to a month.

MAKE THE TART: Warm 2 tablespoons of the olive oil in a medium skillet. Add the onion and thyme sprigs and cook over medium-low heat until the onion is tender and caramelized, about 20 minutes. Remove the thyme stems (most of the leaves will be in the onions) and transfer the onions to a medium bowl.

Meanwhile, warm the remaining 2 tablespoons oil in another medium skillet. Add the mushrooms and cook over medium heat until they have released their juices, about 20 minutes. Stir the mushrooms into the onions.

If you don't have syrup, pour the balsamic vinegar into a small skillet and simmer, uncovered, until reduced to 3 tablespoons, about 5 minutes. Keep an eye on it the last couple of minutes so it doesn't burn.

Whisk the egg and the syrup or reduced vinegar together in a small bowl. Stir in the cheese, $1/2$ teaspoon salt, and a sprinkling of black pepper. Stir into the mushroom mixture.

Preheat the oven to 375°F. Take out the piecrust dough from the refrigerator and let sit at room temperature for at least 15 minutes. Then, either on a lightly floured board or between 2 pieces of parchment paper, roll out the dough, starting from the center and moving outward in all directions. Roll the dough until it is as thin as possible (about $1/16$ inch).

Transfer the dough to the tart pan. Lightly push in the crust to meet the contours of the pan and fold over the edge to fit inside. Fill the pan with the mushroom mixture and bake for 30 to 40 minutes, until the crust is golden and pulls from the sides of the pan. Serve warm or at room temperature.

Roasted Pear and Mixed Greens Salad with Cocoa Nib Windowpane Crisps

*T*HIS SALAD is a wonderful combination of colors, flavors, and textures. The bitter and assertive greens mingle with sweet roasted pears and candied translucent crisps laced with pecans and cocoa nibs. You'll have extra crisps, but they stay crunchy for weeks, covered, at room temperature.

For convenience, wash the greens after they are shredded.

Scharffen Berger cocoa nibs are widely available.

SERVES 6

2 semifirm Anjou or Bartlett pears

¼ cup extra virgin olive oil

2 tablespoons maple syrup

1 tablespoon balsamic vinegar

Salt and freshly ground black pepper

¼ cup sugar, preferably a natural one such as evaporated cane sugar or maple sugar

¼ cup rice syrup

¼ cup chopped pecans

2 tablespoons cocoa nibs

1 small head radicchio

1 small head butter lettuce

1 head arugula, hard stems trimmed, leaves halved

2 tablespoons fresh chives, cut into ¾-inch pieces

Preheat the oven to 400°F. Peel the pears and cut them in half. Core each half, remove the stems, and cut each half into 5 slices. Transfer the pears to a medium bowl and toss with 1 tablespoon olive oil and the maple syrup. Spread the pears on a parchment-covered baking tray and roast about 20 minutes, until tender and starting to brown, turning once or twice. Remove the pears from the oven and lower the temperature to 325°F. Transfer the pears to a bowl and set aside.

(continued)

In a small bowl, whisk together the vinegar, the remaining 3 tablespoons oil, and a sprinkling of salt and black pepper.

MAKE THE CRISPS: Warm the sugar and rice syrup in a small pot until the syrup starts to boil. Stir the sugars to combine and stir in the pecans and nibs. Scoop out the mixture onto a silicone or parchment-covered baking tray and flatten out as best you can. It's thick, but after a few minutes in the oven it spreads thin. Bake for 15 minutes. You can test the sugar's hardness by scooping a bit with a spoon and placing it in a glass of cold water. If it is crisp, it is ready.

Remove from the oven and let the crisp cool, about 10 minutes. Break into irregular-sized pieces and store in a covered container at room temperature.

Shred the radicchio and butter lettuce and place in a bowl with the arugula and chives. You should have about 8 cups of greens. Add the pears and the dressing and toss to combine. Break up the candied pecans and toss a few pieces per serving into the salad. Divide among 6 plates and serve.

Baked Whole Fish in a Salt Crust

*T*HIS IS quite an impressive dish to pull out of the oven. Happily, it is easy to prepare yet elegant enough for a lavish feast. The traditional Mediterranean salt crust seals in moisture and flavor. I wrap the fish in grape leaves before applying the salt to make breaking open the crust quick and neat. The Anchovy Herb Sauce is the crowning touch.

You can prepare the fish and leave them in the refrigerator all day. Take them out 30 minutes before baking.

SERVES 4

I lemon, cut into ⅛-inch rounds
One 1-inch piece of ginger, minced
I garlic clove, minced
½ medium onion, thinly sliced
Salt and freshly ground black pepper

One 2- to 3-pound whole bass, scaled and gutted (or two 1½-pound fish or
　　three 1-pound branzinos)
4 egg whites
½ cup water
2 pounds kosher salt
About 25 jarred grape leaves, rinsed and dried
Anchovy Herb Sauce (recipe follows)

Preheat the oven to 450°F. In a medium bowl, mix together the lemon, ginger, garlic, onion, and a sprinkling of salt and black pepper.

Wash the fish and pat it dry. Place the mixture in the cavity of the fish.

Mix the egg whites with the water and kosher salt in a medium bowl until the salt is thoroughly moistened.

Layer enough grape leaves on a baking tray to cover the length of one fish. Place the fish on the leaves and wrap the leaves up the sides of the fish so the leaves are taut. Place more overlapping leaves on top to encase the fish entirely. Repeat one fish at a time if baking multiple fish. You should be able to get all of the fish on one tray if you place them close together.

Using your hands, cover the fish with a layer of the salt mixture, completely enclosing the fish. The salt should be about ¾ inch deep.

Place the fish in the oven and bake until the salt is browned and the internal temperature is 145°F, about 30 minutes. Two 1½-pound fish cook in 25 minutes; three 1-pound fish take 20 minutes.

Remove the fish from the oven. Break the salt crust with the back of a knife or a mallet. Dust off any salt sticking to the fish. Lift the fish and transfer to a platter. Unwrap the grape leaves, pull back the skin, and lift out the fillets. Serve the fish hot with the Anchovy Herb Sauce drizzled on top.

You can use one 2- to 3-pound fish, two 1½-pound fish, or three 1-pound fish. I favor 1-pound branzinos, a white-fleshed Mediterranean fish, although slightly larger black bass is good too. If you make this with 3 fish, you may need a little more salt mixture to cover the fish entirely. For every extra ½ pound salt, add 2 tablespoons water and 1 egg white.

Anchovy Herb Sauce

*W*ARMING THE anchovies and capers together mellows and marries the flavors of this piquant sauce. It can also be served with lamb, potatoes, and tuna.

MAKES ³/4 CUP

> ¹/2 cup extra virgin olive oil
> 9 flat anchovy fillets, drained, patted dry, and minced
> 2 tablespoons capers, drained, rinsed, and finely chopped
> ¹/2 cup chopped parsley
> I teaspoon fresh lemon juice
> Freshly ground black pepper

Warm the olive oil with the anchovies in a small skillet over medium heat just until warmed. Remove from the heat and stir in the capers.

Transfer to a small bowl and let cool to room temperature. Stir in the parsley, lemon juice, and a generous sprinkling of black pepper.

white Beans and Escarole

*H*ERBED TUSCAN white beans simmered with stock and escarole provide a lush back-drop for the chard gnocchi. The beans can be cooked ahead. Make this with roasted vegetable stock for a scrumptious vegetarian entrée.

SERVES 6

1 ½ cups cannellini beans, soaked overnight
¼ cup extra virgin olive oil
3 garlic cloves, peeled and smashed
1 bay leaf
8 sage leaves
Salt and freshly ground black pepper
4 cups water
2 cups roasted vegetable or chicken stock (pages 4 or 5)
1 head escarole (about ¾ pound), shredded (8 cups)
½ recipe Swiss Chard Gnocchi (recipe follows)
Grated Parmesan cheese (optional)

Drain the beans and place them with the oil, garlic, bay leaf, sage, and 1 teaspoon salt in a medium pot. Add the water, cover, and bring to a boil. Lower the heat and simmer, partially covered, for about an hour, or until the beans are tender. Check from time to time to make sure there is still some water in the pot, and add more if necessary. Sprinkle with a generous amount of black pepper. Taste and add more salt if necessary.

Stir in the stock, escarole, and ¼ teaspoon salt and cover. Bring to a boil, lower the heat, and simmer 15 minutes to marry the flavors. Taste and add more salt and pepper if necessary.

Divide the beans and greens among 6 shallow bowls, top with the gnocchi, sprinkle with the Parmesan, and serve hot.

Swiss Chard Gnocchi

G ORGEOUS GREEN gnocchi are as fun to make as they are to eat. They make a delicious side dish for the fish or a luscious vegetarian entrée with the White Beans and Escarole.

You'll most likely have some extra, so make them ahead and store them frozen. They defrost in 30 minutes and reheat with a quick dip into boiling water. If you like, you can sauté cooked gnocchi in olive oil or butter for a golden crust.

S ERVES 6 AS A MAIN COURSE

2 pounds russet potatoes (about 3 large)
1 teaspoon salt
½ teaspoon freshly ground black pepper
2 bunches Swiss chard (about 1 ¼ pounds), stems and ribs removed
1 large egg
About 1 cup unbleached white flour

Preheat the oven to 400°F. Prick the flesh of the potatoes with a fork and bake until tender, about 1 hour. Peel the potatoes while they are still warm. Mash the potatoes in a large bowl until smooth (if you own a ricer, you can use that) and mix in the salt and black pepper.

Wash the chard by immersing it in a bowl of water. Repeat until there is no grit in the bottom of the bowl. Wilt the chard in a large skillet over medium heat, stirring frequently or tossing with tongs to push the uncooked leaves to the bottom of the pot. You don't have to add water to the pot because the water clinging to the leaves from washing is enough to cook them. Cook until the leaves have wilted, shrunk, and are bright green. Drain and cool the chard. Squeeze out as much excess liquid as possible and finely chop by hand or in a food processor.

Mix the chard into the potato mixture and stir in the egg. Gradually mix in the flour to form a soft, slightly sticky dough.

Bring a 6-quart pot of cold water to a boil and add a tablespoon of salt. Take a piece of dough the size of a golf ball for a tester. Roll out the ball into a 1-inch-wide rope. Cut the rope into ¾-inch-long pieces. Using the floured tines of a fork, lightly press and roll each piece down the length of the tines, forming the gnocchi into an indented curved shape (see illustration opposite). Place the test gnocchi in the boiling water. (Lower the heat under the pot of water to a simmer and cook the gnocchi in simmering water.) When the gnocchi rise to the top after a couple of minutes, wait another 30 seconds or so before removing and testing for consistency. If the gnocchi are fragile and fall apart, add a bit more flour and make another test batch until you have the right consistency and seasoning.

Prepare a floured or a parchment-covered baking tray and set it aside. Divide the full batch of dough into several pieces. Using floured hands, roll each piece into a long rope and cut into pieces. Transfer the gnocchi as you make them to the baking tray.

Boil the gnocchi as described above in 2 batches.

To make the gnocchi the day before, toss them with a little oil after boiling to keep them from sticking to each other. Rewarm them with a dip in boiling water. If freezing, cook them first. Place in a single layer on a baking tray in the freezer. When they are solid, place them in freezer bags. To defrost, lay them in a single layer on a tray for 30 minutes. Dip them in boiling water to warm and serve them with the White Beans and Escarole.

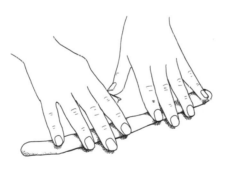

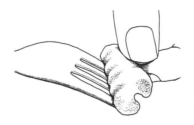

Roasted Cauliflower with Olives and Red Pepper

THIS SIMPLE dish, with its striking colors, complements the other dishes beautifully.

SERVES 4 TO 6

1 medium cauliflower (about 1½ pounds), cut into medium florets (about 7 cups)
1 red bell pepper, cut into slices ½ inch wide and 2 inches long
2 to 3 tablespoons extra virgin olive oil
Salt and freshly ground black pepper
¼ cup pitted kalamata olives, quartered
¼ cup chopped parsley

Preheat the oven to 375°F.

Toss the cauliflower and red pepper in a medium bowl, with just enough oil to coat, ½ teaspoon salt, and a sprinkling of black pepper.

Spread the vegetables on a parchment-covered baking sheet and roast. After 15 minutes, stir. When the cauliflower just starts to turn golden, after another 15 minutes, sprinkle the olives among the vegetables. Return the sheet to the oven and roast an additional 10 minutes or so, until the cauliflower is deeply golden and the olives start to shrivel.

To rewarm, place in a baking dish in a 350°F oven until warmed through. Sprinkle the vegetables with the parsley right before serving. Serve hot.

Semifreddo Affogato

HERE'S A great dessert to keep your guests in the party spirit the whole night long. *Affogato* means "drowned" in Italian. This frozen almondy confection gets doused with hot coffee, preferably espresso, right at the table before eating. Everything but the coffee can be made ahead. The contrasting hot-cold, bitter-sweet, and creamy-crunchy makes an exciting interplay of temperature, flavor, and texture. I like to serve these in oversize coffee mugs.

MAKES TEN 1/2-CUP SERVINGS

I cup whole almonds, chopped

1/4 cup rice syrup

3/4 cup sugar, preferably evaporated cane sugar

4 eggs, separated

I cup blanched almonds

2 cups water

1/2 teaspoon almond extract

1/2 teaspoon vanilla extract

I cup heavy whipping cream

Brewed espresso (1/4 cup per serving)

MAKE THE PRALINE: Preheat the oven to 325°F. Toss the chopped almonds, rice syrup, and 1/4 cup of the sugar together. Spread on a parchment- or silicone-covered baking sheet and bake 20 minutes, mixing halfway through. Remove from the heat and let cool for 15 minutes. Crush into small pieces and set aside. You can do this up to 2 weeks in advance and keep it in a covered container at room temperature.

MAKE THE ALMOND MILK: Have the egg yolks ready in a medium bowl. Blend the blanched almonds and the water together in a blender until smooth. Pour through a cheesecloth-lined strainer (use 4 layers of cheesecloth), squeezing the cheesecloth to extract as much liquid as possible. You should have 2 cups. If you measure a little under 2 cups, add water to make up the difference.

Put the almond milk in a small saucepan with 1/4 cup of the sugar and heat just until

(continued)

scalding, below a boil. Whisking constantly, slowly pour the hot liquid into the bowl of egg yolks. If you pour too quickly, you risk cooking the eggs. Return the mixture to the pot and, stirring constantly, heat just until the mixture is barely thickened, about 5 minutes. Do not let the mixture reach a boil. Remove immediately and pour through a strainer into a medium bowl. Stir in the extracts and let the mixture cool to room temperature.

Whip the egg whites with the remaining $1/4$ cup sugar in a stand mixer fitted with the whisk on medium-high speed until firm peaks form, about 2 to 4 minutes. If you don't have a second stand mixer bowl, carefully scrape the beaten egg whites into another bowl and set aside. Clean out the mixer bowl.

Whip the cream to soft peaks.

Stir a third of the egg whites into the almond milk mixture. Fold in the rest, then in 2 batches fold in the whipped cream. Lastly, fold in the praline.

Ladle the semifreddo into ramekins (the ceramic or 3-inch aluminum kinds are particularly wonderful) and freeze until solid, about 2 to 3 hours.

MAKE THE ESPRESSO: To serve, run a knife around the semifreddo and pop out the dessert into a cup or an oversize coffee mug. Pour 2 to 4 tablespoons of hot espresso over each serving at the table and serve immediately.

Note: The semifreddo stays firm far longer than ice cream, so this is a good choice for a party. You can even travel with the semifreddo for up to an hour.

You can freeze these in whatever container suits your fancy. I love the little disposable aluminum ones that I bake with or $1/2$-cup ceramic ramekins.

New Year's Day

- *Herbed Black-Eyed Peas with Roasted Vegetables* 140

- *Portobello Mushroom Chili with Turkey or Tempeh* 141

- *Avocado-Orange Salsa with Cucumber* 143

- *Old-Fashioned Skillet Corn Bread* 144

- *Gingery Red Cabbage Slaw with Baby Spinach* 145

- *Sweet Potato Pie* 146

- *Cherry-Almond Baked Apples* 149

NEW YEAR'S DAY IS a time to relax and enjoy the start of a bright and promising year. Particularly those who are tired from having stayed up and partied late the night before take pleasure in homey food. This "southern comfort" menu is designed for maximum coziness and flavor and minimum fuss, so you can sit back and recover in front of the Rose Parade or a football game.

It's a common superstition that your luck throughout the year depends on what you eat on January 1. In the South, it's believed that eating black-eyed peas will ensure a year filled with luck, and eating greens, kale, or spinach will make you rich. Others contend that eating corn bread will bring wealth, and cabbage is a "good luck" vegetable whose leaves represent paper currency.

The menu here contains all of those tasty good luck dishes with contemporary flair. Black-eyed peas are cooked with herbs and garlic and simmered with roasted parsnips, rutabaga, and celery root. Old-fashioned Cheddar corn bread bakes in a skillet for a beautiful crust. Gingery Red Cabbage Slaw is flecked with spinach. A rich turkey and portobello chili is topped with an avocado, cucumber, and orange salsa. There's also a delicious vegetarian variation made with tempeh in place of the turkey. Sweet Potato Pie is splashed with a touch of bourbon, and Cherry-Almond Baked Apples make comforting treats that keep well. Every single one of these dishes can be prepared up to several days ahead. You can sleep in and then awake refreshed and prepared to extend a bit of gracious southern hospitality to your grateful family and friends.

Cook's Notes

2 days ahead:

Make the black-eyed peas.
Make the portobello chili with turkey or tempeh.

Prepare the butter piecrust.
Bake the sweet potatoes for the pie.

Day ahead:

Make the corn bread.
Make the Sweet Potato Pie.
Make the red cabbage slaw.
Make the cherry-almond apples.
Make the salsa without the avocado.

Day of:

Add the avocado to the salsa.

Herbed Black-Eyed Peas with Roasted Vegetables

*E*ATING BLACK-EYED peas on New Year's is said to bring good luck for the rest of the year. Here they are cooked with garlic and herbs and simmered with a medley of roasted rutabaga, parsnips, and celery root for a colorful and tasty dish.

It is believed that black-eyed peas originated in India and traveled to the West Indies before making it to America on slave-trading ships. Since they don't grow well in northern climates, they have remained a southern food.

SERVES 6

1 ½ cups black-eyed peas, soaked overnight
6 whole garlic cloves, peeled
2 fresh rosemary sprigs (each about 5 inches long)
6 thyme sprigs
Salt
½ pound rutabaga, peeled and cut into ½-inch dice (1½ cups)
½ pound parsnips, peeled and cut into ½-inch dice (1½ cups)
½ pound celery root, peeled and cut into ½-inch dice (2 cups)
½ pound carrots (4 medium), cut into ½-inch dice (2 cups)
2 tablespoons extra virgin olive oil
Freshly ground black pepper
1 cup finely diced red onion (1 medium)
2 teaspoons fresh lemon juice
¼ cup chopped parsley

Preheat the oven to 400°F. Rinse the peas and place in a medium pot with 6 cups water, the garlic, rosemary, and thyme. Cover, bring to a boil, add 1¼ teaspoons salt, then lower to a simmer. Cook, partially covered, about 40 minutes, until the peas are just tender.

Meanwhile, toss the rutabaga, parsnips, celery root, and carrots with 1 tablespoon of the oil, ½ teaspoon salt, and a sprinkling of black pepper. Spread on a parchment-covered baking tray and roast for about 40 minutes, until tender, stirring every 15 minutes.

Warm the remaining tablespoon olive oil in a medium skillet. Add the onion and sauté over medium heat for 10 minutes, until the onion has colored. Transfer the onion to the peas. Stir in the roasted vegetables and simmer together to marry the flavors for at least 10 minutes. Add a sprinkling of black pepper and the lemon juice. Remove the herb stems (the leaves will have fallen into the beans). Taste and add more salt if needed. Serve hot, sprinkled with parsley.

Portobello Mushroom Chili with Turkey or Tempeh

PORTOBELLO MUSHROOMS and turkey, along with beer and spices, are slowly simmered until all the flavors meld into a deliciously rich chili. For a scrumptious vegetarian version, make the chili with ½ pound of tempeh instead of the turkey (see Note).

SERVES 4

2 ancho chiles

3 tablespoons extra virgin olive oil

1 large onion, cut into small dice (2 cups)

2 garlic cloves, minced

½ pound (2 large) portobello mushrooms, stemmed, caps cut into ½-inch dice (2½ cups)

1 red bell pepper, cut into ¼-inch dice

1 pound ground turkey or ½ pound tempeh

2 teaspoons ground cumin

1 teaspoon dried oregano

1 bay leaf

Salt

One 14-ounce can diced tomatoes

One 12-ounce bottle of beer

1 tablespoon fresh lime juice

Avocado-Orange Salsa with Cucumber (recipe follows)

(continued)

Heat a heavy skillet (preferably cast iron) over a medium flame. Cook the chiles, turning often, until puffed, about 1 minute. Remove from the heat, cut off the stems, tear open the chiles, and discard the seeds. Transfer the chiles to a small bowl and cover with hot water. Set aside.

Warm 1 tablespoon of the oil in a medium pot. Add the onion, garlic, mushrooms, and red pepper. Cook over medium-low heat until the vegetables are very soft and have shrunk way down, about 15 to 20 minutes.

Meanwhile, heat the remaining 2 tablespoons oil in a medium nonstick skillet over medium-high heat. Add the turkey and cook, breaking it up with a spoon and stirring frequently, until no pink remains, about 3 to 5 minutes. Transfer to a bowl and pour off all the liquid.

Put the chiles and 1/4 cup of the soaking liquid into a blender and purée. Set aside. Stir the cumin, oregano, and bay leaf into the sautéed vegetables and cook 1 minute. Add the chile purée. Raise the heat to medium-high and cook, stirring, for an additional 2 minutes.

Transfer the turkey to the pot with the vegetables. Add 2 teaspoons salt, the tomatoes, and the beer. Cover and bring to a boil. Lower the heat and simmer, partially covered, stirring from time to time, for 30 minutes. Uncover and simmer, stirring from time to time, until the chili is thick, about 30 more minutes. Remove and discard the bay leaf. Stir in the lime juice. Taste and add more salt if necessary. Serve the chili hot, with the salsa on top.

Note: Process 1/2 pound tempeh in a food processor until coarsely chopped. You should have 2 cups. Brown the tempeh in the nonstick skillet as you would the turkey.

Avocado-Orange Salsa with Cucumber

THIS WINTER salsa is mellow and sweet but with a playful bite. Dollop it on top of the chili or serve it as a colorful side.

MAKES 2 ½ CUPS

I navel orange

½ cup cucumber, cut into small dice (from a peeled and seeded cucumber)

I jalapeño pepper, stemmed, seeded, and minced

¼ cup minced red onion (½ small onion)

¼ cup chopped fresh cilantro

2 tablespoons fresh lime juice

½ teaspoon salt

I ripe avocado

Cut the peel and any white pith from the orange with a sharp knife, then cut the sections free from the membranes, letting them drop into a medium bowl. Cut the orange sections in half in the bowl to catch the juice.

Add the cucumber, jalapeño, red onion, cilantro, lime juice, and salt.

When you are ready to serve, cut the avocado in half and remove the pit. Holding the avocado half in one hand, make ¼-inch crosshatch cuts through the flesh with a table knife, cutting down to the skin. Separate the diced flesh from the skin by gently scooping out the avocado cubes with a spoon. Add these to the bowl with the rest of the salsa and mix gently. Season with additional salt to taste.

Old-Fashioned Skillet Corn Bread

*H*ERE'S ANOTHER lucky dish to consume on New Year's.

This extra-moist corn bread, laced with Cheddar cheese and corn kernels, is baked in a cast-iron skillet for a beautiful golden crust. If you don't own a cast-iron skillet, make it in an 8 x 8-inch baking dish.

SERVES 8

6 tablespoons butter, melted, plus 1 tablespoon butter, *or* 5 tablespoons coconut oil, melted, plus 1 tablespoon coconut oil

1 cup buttermilk, or 1 cup milk or original flavored soy milk mixed with 2 teaspoons apple cider vinegar

1 cup yellow cornmeal

½ cup unbleached white flour

2 teaspoons baking powder

½ teaspoon baking soda

2 tablespoons maple sugar or Sucanat

½ teaspoon salt

4 scallions, white and green parts, finely chopped (¾ cup)

½ cup grated Cheddar cheese, preferably sharp raw

1 cup corn kernels (frozen is fine)

Preheat the oven to 350°F.

Whisk together the 6 tablespoons melted butter and the buttermilk in a medium bowl.

Whisk together the cornmeal, flour, baking powder, baking soda, sugar, and salt in another medium bowl.

Melt the remaining tablespoon butter in a 9-inch cast-iron skillet over medium heat until browned and bubbling, about 2 minutes.

Pour the wet ingredients into the dry, then whisk the ingredients together until the dry ingredients are completely moistened. Do not overmix. With a spatula or spoon, stir in the scallions, cheese, and corn until just combined.

Immediately spread the batter evenly into the hot pan (the batter will be quite thick) and place in the oven. Bake for 20 minutes, or until the corn bread pulls away from the sides and a toothpick or cake tester inserted into the center comes out clean. Let cool for 30 minutes in the pan before slicing.

Gingery Red Cabbage Slaw with Baby Spinach

ACCORDING TO southern lore, eating cabbage and spinach on January 1 makes you wealthy. This crunchy and refreshing slaw is an especially festive way to ensure prosperity during the coming year.

SERVES 4 TO 6

4 cups thinly sliced red cabbage
1 teaspoon salt
1 medium cucumber, peeled, halved, seeded, and cut into thin slices (about 1 cup)
1 cup packed baby spinach
2 jalapeño peppers, stemmed, seeded, and minced
¼ cup apple cider vinegar
2 teaspoons maple syrup
2 teaspoons minced ginger
Freshly ground black pepper

Mix together the cabbage with the salt in a medium bowl. Place a bowl or plate on top of the cabbage with a weight on top (anything heavy like a can will do) and let sit for 30 minutes to soften the cabbage.

Remove the weight and stir in the cucumber, spinach, and jalapeños.

In a small bowl, mix together the vinegar, maple syrup, ginger, and a sprinkling of black pepper. Stir into the cabbage and let sit for at least 30 minutes to allow the flavors to marry. Serve at room temperature.

Sweet Potato Pie

SATINY SWEET potato pie is made just a bit sophisticated with a touch of orange and brandy. Enjoy this comforting southern treat on New Year's or Thanksgiving.

Stir the coconut milk before measuring, since it separates in the can.

MAKES ONE 9-INCH PIE

2 pounds sweet potatoes (4 medium)
6 gingersnaps (to make ¼ cup crumbs)
½ to ¾ cup maple syrup
½ cup unsweetened coconut milk or heavy cream
½ teaspoon salt
1 tablespoon coconut oil, melted, or butter, melted
¾ teaspoon ground cinnamon
¾ teaspoon ground ginger
¼ teaspoon freshly grated nutmeg
1 teaspoon orange zest
2 tablespoons brandy (optional)
1 whole egg
2 egg yolks
1 recipe single crust (recipe follows) or ½ recipe coconut oil crust (page 51)

Preheat the oven to 350°F. Place the sweet potatoes on an oven rack and bake them about 1 to 1½ hours, or until completely tender when pierced with a fork.

Meanwhile, place the gingersnaps in a food processor and process into crumbs. Set aside.

When cool enough to handle, peel and transfer the sweet potato flesh to a food processor and process until you have a smooth purée. Remove the purée and measure 2 cups. If you like, you can do this step up to 2 days in advance.

Return the measured purée to the food processor and add ½ cup maple syrup, the coconut milk, and the salt. Taste for the desired sweetness and add the extra syrup if necessary. Add the oil, cinnamon, ginger, nutmeg, orange zest, and brandy if desired. Process until smooth. Add the egg and egg yolks and process to mix them in completely. Set aside while you roll the dough.

Have a 9-inch pie plate ready. On a lightly floured board or between 2 pieces of parchment paper, roll out the dough. Start from the center and move outward, rolling the dough until it is as thin as possible (about $1/16$ inch). Transfer the dough to the pie plate. Lightly push in the crust to meet the contours of the plate. Trim the overhang to extend $1/2$ inch beyond the rim of the plate. Fold the overhang under and tuck it in so it is flush with the plate. Make a decorative edge by pressing a piece of the dough between the forefinger of one hand and the thumb and forefinger of the other hand. Repeat this motion continuously around the edge of the entire pie. Press the gingersnap crumbs into the crust halfway up the sides. Let the pie crust cool in the refrigerator for about 30 minutes.

Preheat the oven to 350°F. Place a piece of parchment in the shell and weight the parchment with beans or pie weights. Blind-bake the pie shell for 10 minutes, just enough to firm the crust but not enough to color. Remove the weights and the parchment.

Pour the filling into the pie shell. Bake, uncovered, for about 40 minutes, until the crust is golden brown. Add a collar around the crust (see Note) and bake an additional 10 to 15 minutes, until a knife inserted in the middle comes out clean. Remove the pie from the oven and let it cool to room temperature, at least 2 hours, before cutting.

Note: To make a collar for the crust, take a square piece of foil larger than the pie plate. Fold the piece into quarters. Cut out a quarter circle the size of a quarter of the pie plate. Open up the foil. You should have a square of foil with a cutout circle in the center. Trim off the excess foil at the corners to form a ring. Shape the ring so it will curve over the rim of the piecrust, leaving the filling exposed.

Single Crust

> $3/4$ cup unbleached white flour ($7^1/2$ ounces)
> $1/2$ cup whole wheat pastry flour
> $1/2$ teaspoon baking powder
> $1/4$ teaspoon salt
> $1/4$ cup evaporated cane sugar, maple sugar, or Sucanat
> 1 stick unsalted butter, chilled and cut into small pieces
> 1 teaspoon apple cider vinegar
> 3 tablespoons very cold water

Place the flours, baking powder, salt, and sugar into the bowl of a food processor. Process for a couple of seconds to combine. Add the butter and pulse until the flour and butter become crumbs, about 7 to 10 pulses. The crumbs should be uneven, with some mere crumbs and some the size of small pebbles.

Stir the vinegar into the water. Add the liquid to the food processor and pulse for a couple of seconds just to combine. Do not process until the dough becomes a ball. Turn the dough out onto your work surface and gather it into a rough mass. With the heel of your hand, smear clumps of dough from the center outward about 6 inches to incorporate the butter. You should see striations and the dough will be holding together. Gather the dough into a 4-inch disk and wrap in plastic. Chill the dough for at least an hour before rolling out to let the flour absorb the liquid, firm the butter, and relax the gluten.

Cherry-Almond Baked Apples

*H*ERE'S AN elegant version of a cozy standby. Any dried nut or fruit can be substituted for the almonds or cherries with fine results. A teaspoon of lemon or orange zest is a delicious addition.

SERVES 4

½ cup whole almonds
½ cup dried cherries
¼ teaspoon ground cinnamon
1 tablespoon almond butter
1 tablespoon maple syrup
1 teaspoon vanilla extract
¼ teaspoon almond extract
Salt
4 baking apples, such as Cortland, Rome Beauty, or Mutzu
½ lemon
1 cup apple juice

Preheat the oven to 350°F. Dry-toast the almonds in a medium, heavy-bottomed skillet about 3 minutes, until fragrant and lightly browned. Remove from the heat and chop into small pieces. Place in a bowl with the dried fruit and cinnamon.

Mix together the almond butter, maple syrup, vanilla, almond extract, and a pinch of salt in another small bowl. Stir into the nuts just until the mixture is moistened.

Core the apples and peel a ½-inch band of skin around the middle of each apple to prevent them from splitting. Rub the peeled area with the cut lemon. Spoon about 3 tablespoons of filling into each apple. Place the apples in a baking dish or pie plate and pour the juice on the bottom. Bake, uncovered, until the apples are tender, 45 minutes to an hour, basting every 15 minutes. Serve warm or at room temperature.

Chinese New Year

- Shrimp and Eggplant Dumplings 154
- Sesame Noodles with
  Wilted Napa Cabbage 155
- Crispy Five-Spice Tofu with
  Black Bean Sauce 156
- Five-Spice Roast Chicken with
  Chinese Black Beans 158
- Baby Bok Choy Braised with Mustard Greens
  and Black Mushrooms 159
- Sweet Potatoes with "Happy Berries"
  and Caramelized Walnuts 160
- Almond-Orange Fortune Cookies 162

KUNG HEI FAT CHOI or "congratulations and be prosperous" is the customary greeting at the Chinese New Year, the most significant festival for ethnic Chinese around the world. Abundant symbols and customs revolve around ensuring a year filled with wealth, happiness, good fortune, and longevity.

Based on the lunar calendar, the holiday falls anywhere between late January and late February. Although the public holiday lasts only three days, the celebration traditionally goes on for fifteen, extending from the new moon on the first month of the New Year to the full moon.

Preparations start a month in advance when houses are cleaned, debts are paid, and new clothes are purchased. Homes are decorated with red and gold, considered lucky because, according to ancient Chinese legend, a certain monster could be scared away with liberal use of the bright colors and firecrackers.

On New Year's Eve, all doors and windows are opened to send off the old year. Children and unmarried friends as well as close relatives are given little red envelopes with crisp new bills for good fortune. On this day especially, good behavior is of the essence, for appearance and attitude during the holiday sets the tone for the rest of the year. Parades and colorful lion and dragon dances add to the public festivities.

The celebratory dinner on lunar New Year's Eve is the most important meal of the year. It's customary for loved ones to make a special effort to return home to share in the feast and stay up all night to make the most of the get-together. Feasting is central to this holiday, for lavish amounts of food symbolize abundance and wealth. The foods prepared for these feasts vary, and each family has its own traditions. Many of the dishes made at this time are served because they are regarded as symbols of good luck.

To ensure an auspicious start to the year, gather some friends together and cook up this celebratory feast. Filled dumplings signify good fortune and wealth; long noodles, for "long life," are featured in an appetizer of noodles and cabbage with sesame sauce. A whole chicken, symbolizing wealth for the entire family, is rubbed with five-spice seasoning and roasted with turnips and daikon as good omens. Mustard greens, a "long year vegetable," are braised with bok choy and black mushrooms. The homemade fortune cookies are not only tasty but fun to make and fill with your own personal messages. Finish the feast with mandarin oranges, a lucky symbol since the name of the fruit is phonetically similar to the word for gold.

Cook's Notes

Up to several weeks:

Make the shrimp dumplings and freeze.
Have the fortunes ready to go.

2 days ahead:

Bake the fortune cookies.

1 day ahead:

Make the noodle sauce.
Make the sweet potatoes.
Wash the mustard greens and wrap in a paper towel–lined ziplock bag.

Day of:

Roast the chicken and vegetables.
Make the five-spice tofu.
Braise the greens.
Cook the noodles and toss with the sauce.
Reheat the sweet potatoes.
Steam the dumplings.

Shrimp and Eggplant Dumplings

*T*HESE SAVORY little treasures are considered especially lucky at New Year's. They are also wonderful without the shrimp.

Have everything ready before you start, since this goes together quickly. Freeze the dumplings in a single layer on a baking sheet for an hour or so and stack in freezer bags. Steam them directly from the freezer.

MAKES 44 DUMPLINGS

2 tablespoons sesame oil
$\frac{1}{2}$ pound Japanese eggplant, peeled and cut into small dice (2 cups)
Salt
2 garlic cloves, minced
1 tablespoon minced ginger
2 tablespoons dry sherry
2 tablespoons shoyu
$\frac{1}{2}$ cup water chestnuts, cut into small dice
1 cup bean sprouts
6 tablespoons pine nuts, toasted
$\frac{1}{2}$ pound (12 large) shrimp, shelled, deveined, and chopped small (optional)
2 teaspoons arrowroot powder
One 1-pound package dumpling wrappers, preferably round
Lettuce, to line the steamer
Dipping Sauce (recipe follows)

Warm the oil in a large skillet. Add the eggplant, a sprinkling of salt, the garlic, and the ginger. Cook over medium heat until the eggplant is softened, about 3 minutes. Add the sherry and shoyu and deglaze, stirring until the liquid is absorbed. Stir in the water chestnuts and bean sprouts and cook just until wilted, about 1 minute. Remove from the heat and transfer to a bowl. Stir in the pine nuts, shrimp if using, and arrowroot.

Line a baking sheet with parchment. Have handy a small bowl of water, a pastry brush, and a fork.

Place a wrapper in front of you and brush around the edges with water. Place a heaping teaspoon of filling in the middle of the wrapper. Fold the sides of the wrapper together, pressing a ¹/₂-inch lip around the filling. Press the edges again to make sure the wonton is tightly closed. Place on the prepared baking sheet. Repeat until all the filling is used up.

To cook, steam the wontons over the lettuce-lined steamer for 6 minutes, until translucent around the edges. Serve hot, with the dipping sauce.

Dipping Sauce

Combine 2 teaspoons minced ginger, 2 minced garlic cloves, 2 teaspoons brown rice vinegar, 2 tablespoons dry sherry, 2 tablespoons shoyu, and ¹/₂ cup water in a small bowl.

Sesame Noodles with Wilted Napa Cabbage

UNCUT NOODLES represent long life. Draining the noodles over the cabbage wilts it and transforms it into noodlelike strands, which absorb the flavorful sauce. This dish is delicious served hot or at room temperature.

SERVES 4 TO 6

3 tablespoons creamy peanut butter

2 tablespoons toasted sesame oil

2 tablespoons shoyu

1 tablespoon brown rice vinegar

2 tablespoons mirin or dry sherry

1 tablespoon sugar, preferably evaporated cane sugar or maple sugar

¹/₄ teaspoon hot red pepper flakes or ¹/₂ teaspoon chili sauce

Salt

10 ounces noodles, such as udon, whole wheat spaghetti, or long Chinese noodles

4 cups shredded napa cabbage

¹/₄ cup chopped fresh cilantro

(continued)

In a small bowl, whisk together the peanut butter, sesame oil, shoyu, vinegar, mirin, sugar, and red pepper flakes. Transfer the sauce to a small pot for warming.

Bring a 4-quart pot of water to a boil. Add a sprinkling of salt and the noodles. Cook according to the directions, until al dente.

Meanwhile, place the shredded cabbage in a colander. Gently warm the sauce and have it ready to go.

Drain the noodles in the colander, pouring the hot water over the cabbage, which will just wilt it. Transfer the noodles and cabbage to a large bowl and toss with the heated sauce.

Serve hot, sprinkled with cilantro.

Crispy Five-Spice Tofu with Black Bean Sauce

WHITE FOOD is considered unlucky during the Chinese New Year, so for the best luck, tofu should be pressed or dried rather than left its natural white. The five-spice powder and fermented black soybeans give this crispy tofu dish its distinctive flavor. Both are available in gourmet stores and Asian markets.

SERVES 4

1 pound firm or extra firm tofu

1 tablespoon toasted sesame oil

2 tablespoons chopped fresh ginger

3 garlic cloves, minced

3 tablespoons fermented black beans, rinsed and chopped

2 tablespoons dry sherry or mirin

1 tablespoon shoyu

1 teaspoon sugar, preferably a natural sugar such as evaporated cane sugar or Sucanat

½ teaspoon plus ¼ cup arrowroot powder

¼ cup water

¼ cup thinly sliced scallions, white and green parts

1 tablespoon five-spice powder (see Note)

Unrefined (not toasted) sesame oil or extra virgin olive oil, for sautéing the tofu

Place the tofu on a pie plate and set a second plate on top. Weight the plate with a heavy can and press the tofu for at least 30 minutes.

Meanwhile, warm 1 tablespoon of the toasted sesame oil in a medium skillet. Add the ginger, garlic, and black beans, and sauté 1 minute over medium heat, until sizzling. Stir in the sherry, shoyu, and sugar, and cook 1 minute more. Mix ¹/₂ teaspoon of the arrowroot with ¹/₄ cup water in a small bowl until well combined. Pour into the skillet, stirring constantly for about 1 minute, or until the liquid thickens. Stir in the scallions and set aside.

Drain the tofu. Place the tofu cake on its side and cut it into thirds. Cut the 3 squares diagonally in both directions, forming 12 smaller triangles.

With your fingers, rub the five-spice powder onto both large sides of the tofu.

Spread the remaining ¹/₄ cup arrowroot on a large plate. Film a large nonstick skillet with unrefined sesame oil and warm over medium-high heat.

Dredge each triangle with the arrowroot and immediately lay the pieces in the skillet. (Make sure you hear a sizzle.) Cook 2 to 3 minutes per side, until the tofu is golden and crispy. Serve hot, topped with the black bean sauce.

Note: To make your own five-spice powder, blend together 1 tablespoon star anise, 1 tablespoon ground ginger, 1 tablespoon fennel seed, 1¹/₂ teaspoons ground cloves, and 1¹/₂ teaspoons ground cinnamon.

Five-Spice Roast Chicken with Chinese Black Beans

*W*HOLE CHICKEN symbolizes wealth for the whole family, since "chicken" and "family" sound the same in the Taiwanese dialect. In this dish, Chinese black beans are mixed with garlic and sesame oil, then slipped under the skin, which is rubbed with five-spice powder and Szechuan peppercorns. Turnips and daikon are roasted along with the chicken as good omens.

SERVES 4 TO 6

3 garlic cloves, minced
2 tablespoons fermented black beans, rinsed, drained, and minced
2 tablespoons toasted sesame oil
One 3- to 3½-pound chicken
2 teaspoons Szechuan peppercorns
2 teaspoons five-spice powder (see Note, page 157)
Salt
½ teaspoon hot red pepper flakes or cayenne pepper
1 pound turnips, peeled and cut into 1-inch cubes
½ pound daikon radish, peeled and sliced into ¼-inch diagonals
½ pound carrots, peeled and sliced into ¼-inch diagonals
1 tablespoon extra virgin olive oil

Preheat the oven to 375°F.

Mix the garlic, black beans, and 1 tablespoon of the sesame oil. Use your fingers to tuck the mixture under the chicken breast and thigh skin.

Dry-toast the Szechuan peppercorns in a heavy-bottomed skillet until fragrant, about 2 minutes. Grind the five-spice powder, 1 teaspoon salt, the peppercorns, and red pepper flakes in a spice grinder until finely ground. Rub the mixture all over the chicken.

Place the chicken on a rack in a roasting pan, breast side down. Place the vegetables in a medium bowl and toss with the olive oil plus a sprinkling of salt. Scatter the vegetables around the roasting rack. Roast the chicken for 30 minutes. Remove from the oven. Use wads of aluminum foil or paper towels to flip the chicken breast side up. Brush the remaining tablespoon sesame oil over the chicken and stir the vegetables. Roast for an additional hour or so, until the temperature registers 175°F in the thickest part of the thigh. Let sit for 10 minutes or so to reabsorb the juices. Use a utility scissors or poultry shears to cut up the chicken. Serve hot, with the roasted vegetables.

Baby Bok Choy Braised with Mustard Greens and Black Mushrooms

THE CHINESE call mustard greens "long year vegetable" because they represent long life. In this braise, sweet bok choy mellows their more assertive flavor. The shiitake mushrooms, called black mushrooms in Asian markets, make a tasty stock and add a chewy texture. For best results, try to purchase small bunches of bok choy that weigh about 1/4 pound each.

SERVES 4 TO 6

8 dried Chinese black mushrooms (dried shiitakes)

2 cups water

2 tablespoons shoyu

1 pound baby bok choy (about 4 bunches)

1 tablespoon unrefined sesame oil (not toasted)

1 bunch mustard greens (about 3/4 to 1 pound), stemmed and chopped
   into bite-size pieces

1 medium red bell pepper, cut into 1-inch dice

Place the mushrooms and water in a small pot and bring to a boil. Remove from the heat and let sit for 30 minutes to soften. Drain, reserving the soaking liquid. Stir in the shoyu and set aside.

(continued)

Cut the stems off the mushrooms and discard. Cut the caps into ¼-inch slices. Halve the bok choy lengthwise.

Warm the oil in a large skillet over medium heat. Add the bok choy, cut side down, and cook for about a minute. Add the reserved mushroom liquid, mushrooms, and mustard greens and cover. Simmer for 5 minutes, until the boy choy is almost tender. Sprinkle the bell pepper on top and cook for an additional 5 minutes, until the bok choy and the pepper are quite tender. Remove the lid, turn up the heat, and cook off any remaining liquid, about 5 to 10 minutes. Serve hot.

Sweet Potatoes with "Happy Berries" and Caramelized Walnuts

GINGERY MASHED sweet potatoes are topped with crunchy candied walnuts and studded with bright berries. Goji berries, also known as wolfberries, are a traditional Chinese food that is readily available in natural foods stores and Chinese groceries. Loaded with vitamins and minerals, they are nicknamed the "happy berry" because of the sense of well-being they induce.

Refrigerate extra sweet potatoes in a baking dish and place in a 350°F oven to rewarm.

SERVES 4

I pound sweet potatoes, peeled and sliced into ½-inch rounds
Salt
3 tablespoons sugar, preferably evaporated cane sugar
I cup walnuts, lightly toasted and chopped
2 tablespoons unrefined sesame oil (not toasted)
I tablespoon minced fresh ginger
2 tablespoons maple syrup
¼ cup goji berries, plumped for 5 minutes in hot water (optional)

Cover the sweet potatoes with water in a small pot and add a pinch of salt. Bring to a boil, lower the heat, and simmer until the sweet potatoes are very tender, about 10 minutes. Drain, reserving ¼ cup of the cooking water. Remove to a bowl and mash, adding ½ teaspoon salt and the reserved liquid.

Meanwhile, combine the sugar with 2 tablespoons water in a heavy-bottomed small skillet and cook over medium heat. When the sugar has dissolved, add the walnuts. Stir constantly until the sugar liquid sticks to the walnuts and the walnuts are golden brown, about 5 minutes. Remove from the heat and pour onto a plate. The walnuts will crisp as they cool.

Warm the oil with the ginger and maple syrup in a small skillet. After about 2 minutes, when the ginger becomes fragrant, pour the mixture into the sweet potatoes and stir to combine. Stir in the goji berries if using. Taste and add a pinch more salt if necessary.

Sprinkle with walnuts and serve hot.

Almond–Orange Fortune Cookies

*A*DD A FUN surprise to your New Year's meal and extend blessings and good wishes to your guests in the form of these crispy almond-orange cookies.

Once these cookies come out of the oven, you have to work fast, so before you start, have a muffin tin ready for shaping and your messages prepared on 3 x ½-inch strips of paper. Compose your own or try consulting the *Tao Te Ching* for inspiration. Typical Chinese blessings include "May you enjoy continuous good health" and "May the star of happiness, wealth, and longevity shine on you."

It takes about an hour to make the whole batch. Wear white cotton gloves so you can shape the cookies comfortably.

MAKES 20 COOKIES

¾ cup sliced almonds
2 egg whites
½ teaspoon vanilla extract
¼ teaspoon almond extract
Grated zest of 1 orange
¼ cup plus 2 tablespoons evaporated cane sugar
¼ teaspoon salt
¼ cup whole wheat pastry flour
¼ cup unbleached white flour
2 tablespoons arrowroot powder
2 tablespoons unsalted butter, melted, or 2 tablespoons melted coconut oil

Adjust a rack to the center position of the oven and heat the oven to 400°F. Line 2 cookie sheets with parchment paper.

Dry-toast the almonds in a heavy-bottomed skillet over medium heat, stirring frequently, about 5 minutes. Transfer to a cutting board and chop small. Set aside in a small bowl.

Whisk the egg whites in a medium bowl with the vanilla and almond extracts until foamy. Stir in the zest, sugar, and salt. Sift the flours and arrowroot into the sugar mixture and stir until combined. Stir in the butter and mix well.

Working with one prepared cookie sheet at a time, spoon out a heaping teaspoon of batter. With the back of a spoon working in a circular motion, shape the blob into a 4-inch round. Repeat two more times, keeping them a couple of inches apart. Do not do more than 2 or 3 per cookie sheet, since they have to be formed quickly when the cookies are really hot. (Make 4 per tray if you have a partner with you.) Try to make the cookies as even and round as possible. Sprinkle a border of chopped almonds around the edge of each cookie.

Bake until the cookies are lightly browned, about 5 minutes.

Loosen the cookie from the sheet with a spatula, working quickly. Flip the cookie over and place a fortune in the center. Fold in half enclosing the fortune, to form a semicircle.

Grasp the rounded edges of the semicircle between the thumb and forefinger on one hand. Place the forefinger of the other hand at the center of the folded edge and push in, making certain the solid sides of the cookie puff out.

Place each cookie in a muffin tin until the cookie is set.

Repeat until all of the batter is used up. After the cookies are completely cooled, store in an airtight container for up to a week.

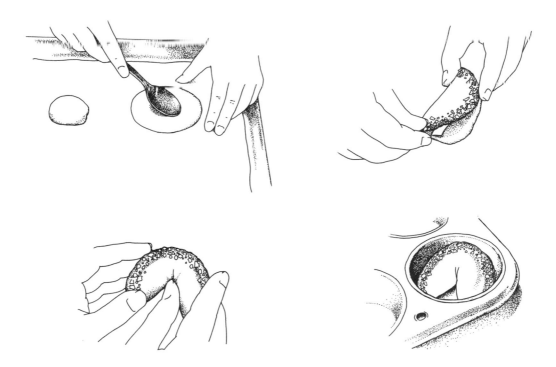

valentine's Day

- *Bruschetta with Salmon Caviar and Chive Spread* 168

- *Fallen Lemon Ricotta Soufflés* 169

- *Endive, Frisée, and Celery Salad with Black Olive Vinaigrette and Sourdough Croutons* 170

- *Breast of Duck with Port-Cherry Sauce* 172

- *Tofu Leek Tart with Sun-Dried Tomatoes and Fresh Herbs* 173

- *Wild Rice and French Lentil Pilaf* 175

- *Meltingly Tender Kale and Escarole* 176

- *Belgian Brownies* 177

VALENTINE'S DAY, undoubtedly the most romantic holiday of the year, has roots that go back thousands of years to the ancient Roman fertility celebration of Lupercalia. In 496, presumably in an attempt to Christianize a rather bawdy pagan festival, Pope Galasius declared the holiday a feast day for the martyr St. Valentine. Soon the day became associated with romantic love, and he became the patron saint of lovers and engaged couples.

A number of colorful legends portrayed St. Valentine as a romantic figure. In one such story, a third-century righteous bishop named Valentine falls in love with his jailor's daughter, cures her of blindness, and sends her a note before his execution signed "From your Valentine."

The first true valentine's card was sent in 1415 by Charles, Duke of Orleans, to his wife from the Tower of London.

Early valentine cards were made by hand, and could be small works of art, decorated with silk, satin, lace, flowers, feathers, or gold leaf. Lonely sailors during the Victorian era made wildly elaborate valentines out of seashells.

The holiday was most likely brought to North America by British settlers. In 1840, Esther Howland, whose father owned a book and stationery store, was inspired by an English valentine to create the first mass-produced valentines out of embossed paper lace. Esther's venture began the greeting card frenzy that we know today. Although perhaps over-commercialized, the holiday is a wonderful opportunity to show people in your life how much you appreciate them, to light the fire for a new flame, or to add a spark of romance to an existing relationship. Send that special someone a card "from your valentine" and don't neglect to cook your way into his or her heart.

This feast is designed for a sensuous winter soirée. Serve a number of friends, cut the recipes down easily for a romantic twosome, or plan on some lovely leftovers. Take one bite into a fallen ricotta soufflé coupled with a wispy salad tossed in an olive vinaigrette and you won't be able to avoid getting into the holiday's spirit. Tender slices of duck or a delicate vegetarian tart pair with a port wine–cherry sauce reduction and individual-sized Belgian Brownies make you feel indulged without being too stuffed for romance. Add some subdued lighting and a bit of your favorite music to complete the mood for a pleasure-filled evening.

Cook's Notes

2 days before:

Make the salad dressing.
Prepare the bread cubes.
Make the Belgian Brownies.
Make the port-cherry sauce.

Day before:

Drain the yogurt.
Prepare the fallen ricotta soufflés.
Press the tart crust into the tart pan.
Prepare the tofu tart filling.
Prepare the wild rice filling stuffing.
Wash the kale and escarole and store in paper towel–lined ziplock bags.

Day of:

Fill the tart and bake.
Prepare the greens for the salad.
Toast the baguette.
Prepare the Meltingly Tender Kale and Escarole.
Cook the duck.
Prepare the Wild Rice and French Lentil Pilaf.
Fold the salmon roe and chives into the yogurt.

Bruschetta with Salmon Caviar and Chive Spread

YOGURT THAT has been drained for 24 hours makes the lightest and most luscious cream cheese. Here, the creamy white base is flecked with chives and brightened with salmon roe pearls. Serve it on slices of toasted baguette for an appetite teaser. Leftovers make a sensuous post–Valentine's Day breakfast.

You can stir in a couple of tablespoons of smoked salmon or trout in place of the salmon roe if you prefer.

MAKES 1 CUP

2 cups plain yogurt
2 tablespoons chives, chopped ¼ inch long
3 tablespoons salmon roe

Small baguette, cut into ¼-inch slices

Drain the yogurt in a cheesecloth-lined strainer over a bowl overnight, up to 24 hours, in the refrigerator. You should have 1 cup.

Transfer the thickened yogurt to a small bowl and stir in the chives. Gently fold in the salmon roe so as not to break the eggs.

Toast the baguette slices and serve with a teaspoon or so of the spread.

Fallen Lemon Ricotta Soufflés

*T*HESE SOUFFLÉS puff when they bake, then settle into luscious savory flans that are removed easily from the ramekins. Serve them on the same plate with the salad for a beautiful presentation. These are perfect to make in advance, and leftovers make a romantic breakfast.

MAKES EIGHT ½-CUP RAMEKINS

3 tablespoons butter, plus more for the ramekins

I cup grated Parmesan cheese (use the large holes on a box grater)

3 tablespoons unbleached white flour

I cup milk

½ cup fresh lemon juice

Grated zest of 2 lemons

4 egg yolks

2 tablespoons snipped chives

Salt and freshly ground black pepper

I cup ricotta cheese, preferably fresh

5 egg whites

Butter eight 3-inch (½-cup) ceramic ramekins and sprinkle them with ½ cup of the Parmesan (about 1 tablespoon per ramekin), pressing the cheese into the sides. Place the ramekins on a baking sheet.

Preheat the oven to 400°F.

Work the 3 tablespoons butter and the flour together to form a thick paste in a small bowl. It's easiest to do this with your fingers.

Bring the milk just to a boil in a small pot. Remove immediately from the heat.

Whisk the paste into the milk to completely dissolve it. Return the pot to the stove, and over low heat, whisking constantly, cook until the base just begins to bubble and thicken, about 1 to 2 minutes. It will be the consistency of soft mashed potatoes.

Remove from the heat and transfer the mixture to a medium bowl. Whisk in the lemon juice, zest, yolks, chives, ¼ teaspoon salt, and a sprinkling of black pepper. Stir in the ricotta and ¼ cup of the Parmesan. Allow the base to cool.

(continued)

In a stand mixer fitted with a whisk or by hand, whip the egg whites to a soft peak, about 1 minute on medium speed. Do not overbeat.

Mix in a quarter of the egg whites to lighten the base.

Fold in the remaining three-quarters of the whites.

Spoon the batter into the prepared ramekins. Sprinkle the top with the remaining ¼ cup grated Parmesan. Bake until the tops are golden, about 15 minutes. Remove from the oven and let the soufflés deflate and cool for about 20 minutes. Run a knife around the sides to unmold the soufflés. You can keep them in the refrigerator for 2 days. Warm them at 350°F until heated through. Serve warm.

Endive, Frisée, and Celery Salad with Black Olive Vinaigrette and Sourdough Croutons

THIS SALAD is a mélange of exciting flavors and textures. The dressing is delicious with or without the anchovies.

SERVES 6 (MAKES 1 CUP DRESSING)

Bread Cubes
3 cups large (¾- to 1-inch) sourdough bread cubes

1 tablespoon extra virgin olive oil

Dressing
1 tablespoon fresh lemon juice

2 tablespoons red wine vinegar

2 garlic cloves

6 tablespoons extra virgin olive oil

Freshly ground black pepper

3 anchovy fillets (optional)

1 cup pitted kalamata olives, finely chopped

¼ cup chopped parsley

Salad

> 4 cups frisée leaves, from 1 large head frisée or 2 small (¾ pound)
> 2 heads Belgian endive (½ pound)
> 2 celery stalks

Preheat the oven to 350°F.

In a medium bowl, toss the bread cubes with the olive oil. Spread on a baking sheet and bake about 15 minutes, until lightly browned and crispy. Remove from the oven and set aside.

Combine the lemon juice, vinegar, garlic, olive oil, a sprinkling of black pepper, and the anchovies, if using, in a blender and blend until smooth. Stir in the olives and parsley.

Pull the tender leaves off the frisée, leaving the thick white stems behind. Remove the leaves from the endive and slice the leaves into thin spears. You should have 3 cups. Cut the celery into thirds (about three 3-inch-long pieces). Cut each piece lengthwise into thin slices. You should have about 1 cup.

Soak the leaves and the celery in cold water for at least 15 minutes to crisp. Drain, dry, and place in a large bowl.

Toss the greens with the dressing and the croutons. Divide the salad among 6 plates.

Breast of Duck with Port–Cherry Sauce

THIS ROMANTIC love potion of a sauce complements the pilaf and tart as well as the duck. Although I favor sherry vinegar, port wine, and a homemade stock, you can substitute red wine vinegar, a boxed stock, and mixed berry juice and turn out a tasty sauce.

SERVES 4 TO 6

$\frac{1}{2}$ cup minced shallots
$\frac{1}{2}$ cup sherry vinegar
4 cups chicken or roasted vegetable stock (pages 5 or 4)
$\frac{1}{2}$ cup port
1 cup dried cherries
1 tablespoon Dijon mustard
Salt and freshly ground black pepper
2 boneless magret duck breast halves

Simmer the shallots and vinegar in a medium skillet over medium heat until almost dry, about 5 minutes. Add the stock, port, and cherries. Bring to a boil. Lower the heat and reduce at a rapid simmer until you have 2 cups, about 25 minutes. Whisk in the mustard and sprinkle with $\frac{1}{4}$ teaspoon salt and a sprinkling of black pepper. Set aside while you make the duck.

Trim off any overhanging fat on the duck. Score the skin side of the duck into the fat in a $\frac{3}{4}$-inch crisscross, being careful not to cut into the flesh.

Heat a large, heavy-bottomed skillet over medium-high heat and add the duck breasts, skin side down. You should hear a nice sizzle. Lower the heat to medium and cook for 15 minutes on the first side, until most of the fat is rendered and the skin is crispy and deep golden.

Pour off most of the fat, leaving only a thin film. Flip the duck breasts and cook 10 minutes on the second side.

Remove from the pan, tent the duck with foil, and let rest for 5 minutes. Slice into $\frac{1}{2}$-inch angled pieces and serve with the cherry sauce.

Tofu Leek Tart with Sun-Dried Tomatoes and Fresh Herbs

THIS SAVORY tart has a rich pine nut crust and a delicate, herbed filling. The flavors marry beautifully with the cherry sauce from the duck.

You can also make 5 individual 4-inch tartlets in place of the whole tart. If you like, play around with the herb combination and add extra basil or a mixture of parsley and thyme.

MAKES ONE 9-INCH TART (SERVES 6)

Crust

½ cup pine nuts

1 cup whole wheat pastry flour

¼ teaspoon baking powder

2 tablespoons extra virgin olive oil

¼ cup milk or original flavored soy milk

Pinch of salt

Filling

¼ cup extra virgin olive oil

3 cups chopped leeks, white part only

1 pound firm or extra firm tofu, drained and cut into 1-inch cubes

2 tablespoons fresh lemon juice

1 medium garlic clove, minced

2 teaspoons light miso, such as white or mellow barley

¾ teaspoon salt

Freshly ground black pepper

2 tablespoons chopped fresh tarragon

2 tablespoons chopped fresh basil

¼ cup sun-dried tomatoes, (not in oil) (about 7),
    reconstituted and cut into ¼-inch slices (see Note)

1 cup bread crumbs, preferably fresh from whole wheat bread

(continued)

Preheat the oven to 350°F.

MAKE THE CRUST: Grind the pine nuts in a food processor with the flour and baking powder until floury. The flour will keep the nuts from turning into paste. Transfer to a medium bowl.

Whisk the oil, milk, and salt in small bowl. Add to the flour mixture, stirring until the dry ingredients are completely moistened.

Place a piece of plastic wrap between your fingers and press the crust into an oiled 9-inch tart pan or five 4-inch tart pans. Press the last few times with your thumb around the sides where the bottom of the pan meets the side to make sure there is no excess crust there. Use a knife to cut off any excess along the top of the tart pan, and poke holes all over the crust with the tines of a fork. Bake the shell for 5 minutes, then remove from the oven and set aside. Do not turn off the oven.

MAKE THE FILLING: Warm 1 tablespoon of the olive oil in a medium skillet. Add the leeks and cook 6 to 8 minutes over medium-low heat, until the leeks have softened and sweated and are only lightly browned. Set aside.

In a pot of boiling, lightly salted water, cook the tofu at a gentle simmer for 5 minutes. Remove the tofu from the water with a slotted spoon, place on paper towels to absorb the excess water, and pat dry. Place in a medium bowl.

Place the remaining 3 tablespoons olive oil, the lemon juice, garlic, miso, salt, and a sprinkling of black pepper in a small bowl and whisk to combine. Pour into the bowl with the tofu and use a potato masher or fork to mash the flavorings into the tofu until the tofu has absorbed all the liquid and has turned into curds. Stir in the fresh herbs, sun-dried to- matoes, and bread crumbs. Mix in the leeks. Spread the filling evenly over the crust in the tart pan.

Bake approximately 40 minutes, until the tofu is firm and the crust has lightly browned.

Remove from the oven and let sit for a couple of minutes. Carefully push the tart out of the tart pan while it is still hot. Serve immediately.

Note: Pour hot water over the tomatoes and let sit for 10 minutes to soften.

wild Rice and French Lentil Pilaf

DICED SUNCHOKES, also known as Jerusalem artichokes, add brightness and a delicate crunch to the fluffy herb-scented pilaf. Tiny French lentils are especially elegant here. Although it may be served at room temperature, a quick steam reheats this dish beautifully.

SERVES 6

½ cup French lentils
½ cup wild rice
5 cups water
¾ teaspoon salt
1 bay leaf
1 fresh rosemary sprig
6 whole fresh sage leaves, plus 1 tablespoon chopped fresh sage
2 tablespoons extra virgin olive oil
½ cup minced shallots
½ pound sunchokes (Jerusalem artichokes), peeled and diced small (1 heaping cup)
Freshly ground black pepper

Rinse the lentils and rice and put them in a medium pot with the water, salt, bay leaf, rosemary, and whole sage leaves. Cover and bring to a boil. Lower the heat and cook, partially covered, until the lentils and rice are tender and some of the rice kernels have burst open, 45 to 50 minutes. Cook, uncovered, another 10 minutes or so to cook off some of the excess liquid. Remove the bay leaf and rosemary sprig and drain any remaining liquid.

Warm the olive oil in a medium skillet. Add the shallots and sunchokes and sauté over medium heat just until the shallots brown and the sunchokes are still crisp-tender, about 5 minutes.

Stir the sunchokes and shallots into the cooked lentils and rice along with the tablespoon of chopped sage. Sprinkle with black pepper. Taste and add more salt if necessary. Serve hot. To reheat, steam until heated through.

Meltingly Tender Kale and Escarole

*W*HAT A PLEASURABLE way to enjoy invigorating greens! Use the more delicate kale, often called lacinato, Tuscan, or black kale, if you can find it.

SERVES 2 TO 4

2 tablespoons extra virgin olive oil
1 medium onion, minced (1 cup)
1 red bell pepper, cut into small dice (1 cup)
1 medium head escarole (¾ pound), leaves rinsed and chopped (see Note)
1 large head kale (1 pound), preferably black kale (Tuscan kale), stemmed, leaves rinsed
    and chopped (see Note)
2 garlic cloves, minced (2 teaspoons)
Salt and freshly ground black pepper

Heat the oil in a large, deep skillet over medium-high heat. Add the onion and bell pepper, and cook, stirring often, 5 minutes or until softened. Add the escarole, kale, and garlic, and cook, tossing often, over medium heat until wilted, about 4 minutes.

Add ½ cup water and cook 5 to 10 minutes, or until almost dry. Stir in another ½ cup water and cook 5 to 10 minutes, or until almost dry. Add another ½ cup water and simmer 5 minutes more. The greens should be tender and moist but not soupy. If not tender, cook a bit longer in a little more liquid. Season to taste with salt and black pepper. Serve hot.

Note: Chop the leaves into pieces and then wash. It's okay to have water clinging to the leaves.

Belgian Brownies

*T*HESE INDIVIDUAL confections puff like soufflés before they settle down into chocolate ambrosia. With chocolate chips oozing in the middle and crackly sugar around the sides, these romantic, wheat-free treats taste decadent but won't weigh you down.

The brownies stay moist for days, making them ideal to prepare in advance. They are easily transportable and work for birthdays and picnics as well as sexy soirées.

MAKES **10** BROWNIES

6 tablespoons butter or coconut oil, plus more for oiling the cups

3 tablespoons plus ½ cup sugar, preferably maple or evaporated cane sugar

6 ounces semisweet chocolate, coarsely chopped

4 large eggs

1 teaspoon vanilla extract

¼ teaspoon salt

6 tablespoons oat flour or ¼ cup chickpea flour

1 cup semisweet chocolate chips

Adjust the oven rack to the center position in the oven and preheat the oven to 400°F. Generously butter or oil 10 ramekins. (The 3-inch aluminum disposable variety are especially wonderful here because they make it so easy to pop out the brownies when they're done.) Pour 3 tablespoons of sugar into the first one. As you rotate the ramekin to coat the sides, pour the excess into the next. Continue until all the ramekins are sugar coated, adding more sugar as necessary. Place the ramekins on a baking sheet.

Meanwhile, melt the butter or oil and the 6 ounces chocolate in a small pot until the chocolate is almost melted. Remove from the heat and stir until completely melted and smooth. Scrape into a medium bowl to cool.

Place the eggs, vanilla, salt, and remaining ½ cup sugar in a stand mixer fitted with the whisk attachment. Beat at the highest speed until the volume nearly triples, the color is very light, and the mixture drops from the beaters in a smooth, thick stream, about 4 to 5 minutes. Scrape the egg mixture over the melted chocolate and sprinkle the flour over the egg mixture. Gently fold the egg and flour into the chocolate until the mixture is uniformly colored.

(continued)

Ladle a $1/2$-inch layer of batter into each ramekin. Sprinkle a layer of chocolate chips evenly among the ramekins, about 1 heaping tablespoon each. Ladle the remaining batter evenly over the chips.

Bake for 12 to 13 minutes. The brownies should be firm on top and dry to the touch but still moist in the middle. A toothpick inserted $1/2$ inch from the side should come out clean.

Remove from the oven and let sit in the ramekins until cooled to room temperature, at least 20 minutes. They will sink down considerably. Invert the brownies to dislodge them. Turn right side up to serve. Store, covered, at room temperature for up to 5 days.

Note: I use Florida crystals (evaporated cane sugar) for the sides and maple sugar for the batter. Florida crystals give the crust a crackly crunch.

I generally make these with oat flour, but chickpea flour makes this a delicious gluten-free dessert.

St. Patrick's Day

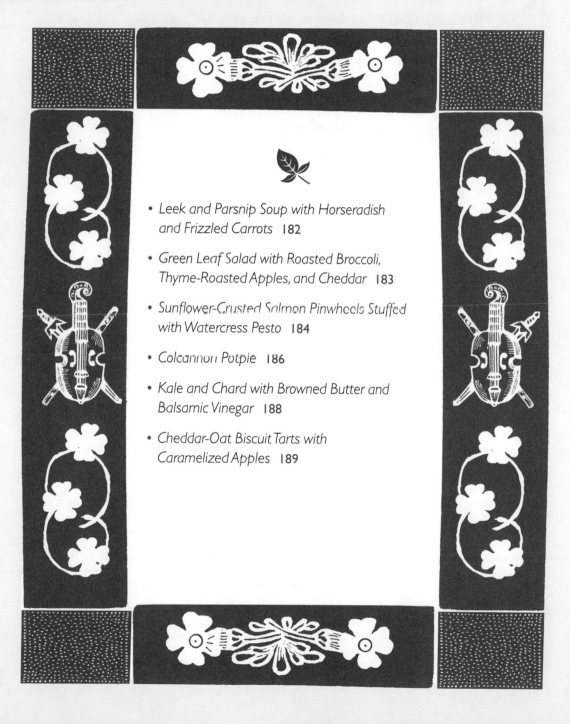

- Leek and Parsnip Soup with Horseradish and Frizzled Carrots 182

- Green Leaf Salad with Roasted Broccoli, Thyme-Roasted Apples, and Cheddar 183

- Sunflower-Crusted Salmon Pinwheels Stuffed with Watercress Pesto 184

- Colcannon Potpie 186

- Kale and Chard with Browned Butter and Balsamic Vinegar 188

- Cheddar-Oat Biscuit Tarts with Caramelized Apples 189

T. PATRICK'S DAY is observed in America on March 17. Although a Catholic religious holiday in Ireland, in the United States it is more of a secular celebration, widely embraced by Americans of Irish descent as well as non-Irish. It is a day of parades, music, feasting on Irish food, whiskey and beer, and wearing green. The "wearing of the green" not only symbolizes the birth of springtime but is said by Irish legend to attract fairies and promote flourishing crops.

St. Patrick himself, born of English descent, is believed to have died on March 17. He is credited with converting large numbers of Celtic pagans to Christianity and with bringing the Latin alphabet to Ireland. The religious holiday in Ireland is a traditional day for offering prayers to missionaries worldwide. St. Patrick is said to have incorporated traditional Irish symbols and customs to teach Christianity, and is said to have used the shamrock, the Irish three-leaved clover, as a symbol of the Trinity. He superimposed the Celtic sun symbol over the cross, creating the singular Celtic cross.

Long before Irish cuisine became associated with the ubiquitous potato, the diet was healthy and diverse. The Druids harvested a wide variety of vegetables including rutabagas, parsnips, cabbage, kale, leeks, scallions, and onions, as well as making use of the sheep and cattle that grazed in lush pastures, and fish from coastal waters. Since the industrialization of farming largely bypassed Ireland in the late nineteenth century, much of the country's traditional agricultural practices remained intact. Ireland, however, underwent a pronounced technical and economic resurgence in the 1980s and 1990s, and earned the nickname "Celtic Tiger" for having one of the fastest-growing economies of Europe.

An excellent modern cuisine is currently emerging out of Ireland based on the highest-quality ingredients. Old favorites and ingredients are being revisited, often with new techniques and a lighter touch. The fertile pastures make for some of the most flavorful dairy in the world. The potato is still beloved, and to this day, many dishes revolve around the old standby.

The menu here celebrates Irish ingredients and dishes. The parsnip-potato soup, spiked with horseradish, has a festive flourish of roasted carrot curls. A green leaf salad includes tart apples and farmhouse Cheddar. The main course of salmon pinwheels stuffed with watercress pesto baked on a bed of leeks features what has long been regarded by the Irish as the king of fish. A colcannon crust of potatoes and cabbage tops two versions of a pot-pie, one chicken and one vegetarian. Luscious kale drizzled with browned butter and individual tarts with oat biscuit crusts and caramelized apples round out the feast. A hearty stout is an excellent accompaniment.

Whether you are of Irish descent or not, it's great fun to celebrate and become Irish for a day. Cook and feast the Irish way, play some Irish music, try out some Irish words, tell a few Irish jokes, and make merry the whole night long. Be sure to wear green.

Cook's Notes

2 days in advance:

Make the soup.
Make the salad dressing.

1 day in advance:

Make the watercress pesto.
Make the Colcannon Potpie.
Wash the greens.
Caramelize the apples for the biscuit tart.

Day of:

Roast the apples and broccoli for the salad.
Prepare the salad greens.
Prepare the salmon pinwheels and bake the salmon.
Assemble the biscuit and bake the tarts.
Roast the garnish for the soup.
Cook the kale and chard.
Reheat the Colcannon Potpie.

Leek and Parsnip Soup with Horseradish and Frizzled Carrots

*I*N THIS VARIATION on a leek and potato soup, the horseradish makes this soup sing, and the bright and crinkly carrots elevate it from rustic to festive.

SERVES 4 TO 6

½ pound carrots (2 medium), peeled

3 tablespoons extra virgin olive oil

Salt

3 cups small diced leeks, white and light green parts only

2 garlic cloves, minced

¼ teaspoon hot red pepper flakes

I pound parsnips, peeled and cut into ½-inch dice

½ pound thin-skinned potatoes, peeled and cut into ½-inch dice

4 cups vegetable stock (page 4 or 6) or water

Freshly ground black pepper

I tablespoon prepared horseradish

I teaspoon fresh lemon juice

¼ cup chopped fresh dill, plus more for garnish

Preheat the oven to 375°F. Use a vegetable peeler to peel carrot strips the length of the carrots. In a medium bowl, toss the carrots with 1 tablespoon of the olive oil and ¼ teaspoon of salt. Transfer to a parchment-covered baking tray and roast, stirring every 10 minutes, until the carrots are crispy and curled (removing the ones that are browned after 30 minutes), about 40 minutes. Remove from the oven and store in a container at room temperature.

Meanwhile, warm the remaining 2 tablespoons oil in a medium pot. Add the leeks and sauté over medium-low heat until softened but not browned, about 7 minutes. Add the garlic and red pepper flakes and sauté an additional 2 minutes. Add the parsnips, potatoes, stock, and 1½ teaspoons salt. Cover, raise the heat, and bring to a boil. Lower the heat and simmer, partially covered, until the vegetables are tender, about 20 minutes. Use the back of a spoon to smash half of the vegetables against the sides of the pot to thicken the broth. Stir in a generous sprinkling of black pepper, the horseradish, lemon juice, and dill. Taste and add more salt if necessary. Serve hot, sprinkled with fresh dill and topped with a mound of carrot curls.

Green Leaf Salad with Roasted Broccoli, Thyme-Roasted Apples, and Cheddar

SOME OF the world's best Cheddars come out of Ireland. The contrasting flavors and textures of the ingredients in this salad are enhanced by the sweet-tart dressing and tangy cheese.

SERVES 6

3 Granny Smith apples
6 tablespoons extra virgin olive oil
1 tablespoon minced fresh thyme
Salt and freshly ground black pepper
1 pound broccoli, cut into small florets (4 cups)
1 tablespoon fresh lemon juice
1 tablespoon red wine vinegar
1 ½ teaspoons honey
1 tablespoon Dijon mustard
1 garlic clove, minced
1 head green leaf lettuce (¾ pound), washed and torn into bite-sized pieces (8 cups)
1 cup grated Cheddar cheese, preferably sharp raw

Preheat the oven to 375°F. Core, peel, and cut the apples into quarters, then cut each quarter into 3 wedges. Toss the apples in a medium bowl with 1 tablespoon of the oil, the thyme, ¼ teaspoon salt, and a sprinkling of black pepper. Spread on a parchment-covered baking tray and bake until golden and tender, turning once, about 30 minutes.

Toss the broccoli in a medium bowl with 1 tablespoon of the oil, ¼ teaspoon salt, and a sprinkling of black pepper. Spread on a parchment-covered baking tray and roast until deeply golden, turning once, about 30 minutes.

In a small bowl, whisk together the lemon juice, vinegar, honey, mustard, garlic, and ¼ teaspoon salt. Whisk in the remaining 4 tablespoons of oil until emulsified.

Toss the lettuce with the apples, broccoli, cheese, and dressing. Divide among 6 plates and serve.

Sunflower-Crusted Salmon Pinwheels Stuffed with Watercress Pesto

THIS ELEGANT dish looks challenging but is actually quite simple to prepare.

You may have some pesto left over. It is delicious dolloped on pasta, potatoes, and bread. Since you need 1 cup of sunflower seeds in total for the fish and the pesto, toast all the seeds at once and divide them.

Use a center-cut piece of salmon so that the pieces are of even thickness.

SERVES 6

Pesto

½ cup sunflower seeds
4 cups watercress, heavy stems removed (from 2 large bunches), washed and dried
6 tablespoons extra virgin olive oil
¾ teaspoon salt
Freshly ground black pepper
2 garlic cloves
2 tablespoons fresh lemon juice

Fish

½ cup sunflower seeds
1 tablespoon extra virgin olive oil
3 cups chopped leeks, white and light green parts only
One 1½-pound piece salmon fillet, skinned
Salt and freshly ground black pepper
1 bunch fresh watercress, well washed and dried, heavy stems removed, leaves torn off

Dry-toast the sunflower seeds for both the pesto and the fish in a heavy-bottomed skillet until golden, about 3 minutes.

MAKE THE PESTO: Place ½ cup sunflower seeds, the 4 cups watercress, the olive oil, salt, a sprinkling of black pepper, the garlic, and the lemon juice in a food processor. Process until smooth, scraping down the sides as necessary. Store refrigerated and covered for up to 4 days.

MAKE THE FISH: Place ½ cup sunflower seeds in a food processor and pulse just to chop coarsely. Transfer the sunflower seeds to a small plate.

Preheat the oven to 450F. Warm the oil in a medium skillet. Add the leeks and sauté over medium heat until softened, about 5 minutes. Transfer to a baking dish (8 x 11 inches is ideal) and spread the leeks out evenly. Sprinkle with salt and black pepper. Cut the salmon into 6 pieces about 1 inch wide and butterfly open to make a long piece. Lightly sprinkle the pieces with salt and pepper. (See the illustrations below.) Spread with a thin layer of pesto and roll into a pinwheel shape. Dredge the salmon on both sides in the sunflower seeds. Place the medallions over the leeks.

Bake for 12 minutes, until light pink in the middle. Serve the medallions with the leeks on a bed of fresh watercress leaves.

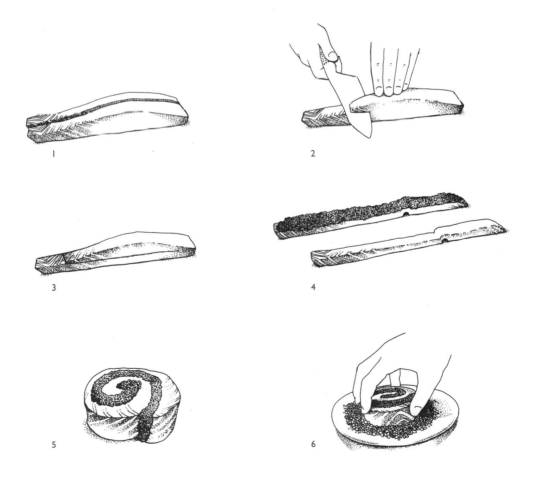

colcannon Potpie

COLCANNON IS a traditional Irish dish that combines mashed potatoes and wilted kale or cabbage. This potpie with a colcannon top crust can be made with either seitan, for vegetarians, or chicken.

SERVES 6 TO 9

Topping

 1 pound russet potatoes, peeled and cut into 1-inch cubes

 Salt

 1 tablespoon extra virgin olive oil

 1 onion, thinly sliced

 3 cups shredded cabbage

 1/4 cup milk or original flavored soy milk

 1 tablespoon butter

Filling

 3/4 pound seitan, cut into 1/2-inch chunks, or 3/4 pound boneless chicken breasts, cut into 1-inch chunks (about 1 1/2 to 2 cups)

 3 tablespoons unbleached white flour

 2 tablespoons extra virgin olive oil

 1/2 pound shiitake mushrooms, stems removed and caps thinly sliced (4 cups)

 1 tablespoon shoyu

 3 garlic cloves, minced

 1 red bell pepper, cut into 3/4-inch cubes

 1 1/2 teaspoons dried thyme

 1/2 teaspoon dried marjoram

 1/2 pound turnips, peeled and cut into 3/4-inch cubes (1 1/2 to 2 cups)

 3/4 cup red wine

 1 cup vegetable or chicken stock (pages 4 to 6)

 2 tablespoons tomato paste

 Salt and freshly ground black pepper

 1 cup fresh or frozen peas

MAKE THE TOPPING: Put the potatoes in a medium pot with water to cover. Add 1 teaspoon salt, bring to a boil, and cook until softened, about 10 minutes.

Meanwhile, warm the oil in a medium skillet. Add the onion and cabbage and cook over medium-low heat until softened, about 15 minutes.

When the potatoes are cooked, drain the liquid, reserving 1/4 cup of cooking liquid. Add the milk, butter, the reserved liquid, and 1/2 teaspoon salt to the potatoes and mash until smooth. Stir in the sautéed onion and cabbage and set aside.

Preheat the oven to 350°F.

MAKE THE FILLING: Dredge the seitan or chicken in the flour.

Warm the olive oil in a large skillet over medium heat. Add the seitan or chicken and cook until browned, about 2 minutes per side. Remove the seitan or chicken from the pan and set aside.

Add the mushrooms and shoyu, scrape up any brown bits, and cook until softened, about 10 minutes. Add 2 tablespoons of water if it's too dry. Stir in the garlic, bell pepper, thyme, and marjoram and cook another 3 minutes. Add the reserved seitan or chicken, the turnips, wine, stock, and tomato paste, along with 1/2 teaspoon salt and a sprinkling of black pepper. Bring to a boil, then lower the heat to a rapid simmer. Cook about 10 minutes, stirring from time to time until the vegetables are softened and the stock is thick. Stir in the peas and cook another 3 minutes. Taste and add additional salt if necessary.

Pour the vegetables into an 8 x 8-inch baking dish. Spread the mashed potato topping over the top and bake for 30 minutes, until the topping is firm and golden. Remove from the oven and let sit for 5 to 10 minutes to firm before serving.

Kale and Chard with Browned Butter and Balsamic Vinegar

KALE IS an Irish staple. Here the hearty green is combined with the sweeter and more tender chard and tossed with balsamic vinegar and butter, which has been heated until it turns fragrant and nutty.

SERVES 6

2 large bunches kale, stemmed and chopped into bite-sized pieces
1 bunch Swiss chard, preferably red, stemmed and chopped into bite-sized pieces
Salt and freshly ground black pepper
2 tablespoons butter
1 tablespoon balsamic vinegar

Wash the greens after they are cut, and drain them. Place a large, deep skillet over medium heat and add the greens, a handful at a time, until they all fit in the pot. Use tongs to toss the greens as they start to wilt. The water clinging to the leaves should be enough to wilt them.

Keep cooking, stirring from time to time, until the greens are fully wilted and tender, about 15 minutes. You may have to add some water for the last 5 minutes of cooking. Sprinkle the greens with salt and black pepper.

In a small pot, melt the butter and let it cook until it is browned and fragrant, about 3 minutes. Remove from the heat and stir in the vinegar. Immediately pour over the greens and stir to combine thoroughly. Serve hot.

Cheddar-Oat Biscuit Tarts with Caramelized Apples

CARAMELIZED APPLES and toasted walnuts are baked into individual tartlike biscuits. Warm just before serving and top with a scoop of ice cream. Any leftover tarts make delicious breakfast treats.

These can be made in advance, frozen, defrosted, and reheated at 350°F.

MAKES SIXTEEN 4-INCH TARTS

Filling

2½ pounds baking apples (7 medium), such as Granny Smith or Golden Delicious

6 tablespoons (¾ stick) unsalted butter

½ cup sugar, preferably natural sugar such as evaporated cane sugar or maple sugar

½ cup walnuts, toasted and chopped

Biscuit

1 cup whole wheat pastry flour

½ cup unbleached white flour

¼ cup sugar, preferably natural sugar such as evaporated cane sugar or maple sugar

2 teaspoons baking powder

½ teaspoon baking soda

½ teaspoon salt

¾ cup rolled oats

6 tablespoons (¾ stick) unsalted butter, cut into pieces

1½ cups grated sharp Cheddar cheese

1 egg

½ cup plus 2 tablespoons buttermilk (see Note)

Vanilla or caramel ice cream, for serving

MAKE THE FILLING: Peel and core the apples. Cut each apple into 12 even wedges. In a large skillet, melt the butter over medium-high heat. When it is hot but not smoking, add the

(continued)

apples and sprinkle on the sugar. Stir the apples just until the sugar is melted, then leave the apples cooking without stirring for 5 minutes. Flip them and leave them for another 5 minutes. Turn the heat to medium (the apples should be a nice caramel color by now) and cook until softened, flipping a couple of times, about 5 to 7 more minutes. Stir in the nuts and remove from the heat.

Preheat the oven to 425°F.

MAKE THE BISCUIT: Pulse together the flours, sugar, baking powder, baking soda, salt, and oats in a food processor.

Add the butter and pulse until the mixture is coarse crumbs. Add the cheese and pulse to combine.

Pour the mixture out into a medium bowl.

Combine the egg and buttermilk and stir gently into the flour mixture just until combined.

Turn the dough out onto a floured surface and knead gently, about 6 turns. Divide the dough into 16 pieces. Press each piece into a disk about ¼ inch thick. Arrange 5 wedges of apple per biscuit. Transfer the biscuits to a parchment-covered baking sheet. Bake approximately 12 to 14 minutes, until the bottom is deep golden brown. Remove from the oven and let cool slightly. Serve warm, with a scoop of ice cream.

Note: Substitute milk or soy milk with 2 teaspoons lemon juice for the buttermilk. Let sit for 5 minutes to clabber.

Passover

THE MOST WIDELY OBSERVED and beloved of all Jewish holidays, Passover commemorates the release of the Jews from bondage under the pharaohs of Egypt thirty-three centuries ago. The story is retold and celebrated each year during the Passover meal, or seder. The eight-day holiday falls anywhere from late March through the end of April, depending on the lunar calendar. *Seder* means "order," and refers to the festive feast and the ceremony that takes place on the first two nights of the holiday. Family and friends gather to participate in the occasion, which often goes late into the night.

The Haggadah, the text read during the seder, recounts the story of the exodus of the Jews from slavery in Egypt to freedom. For the modern person, "going out of Egypt" represents the endeavor to liberate oneself from places where one is "stuck." On the way to individual liberation, one often finds there is a period of "wandering in the desert." The holiday is also referred to as the Season of Our Freedom, for true freedom is freedom from limitation, whether the limitation is external and physical, or internal and psychological, or spiritual.

The holiday is known also as the holiday of matzo. Since the Israelites had to leave Egypt in a hurry without enough time to leaven the bread, no foods with any leavening are consumed for the duration of the holiday. Specifically, that means nothing containing wheat, spelt, barley, rye, and oats. Matzo, a crispy ritual flatbread, is consumed during the seder and for the duration of the holiday. Ashkenazic Jews, those who originated from Eastern Europe, include millet, corn, rice, and legumes in the list of prohibited foods.

Since Jewish Americans trace their ancestry to a variety of cultures, traditional foods for the seder meal vary widely. The menu in this book reflects an eclectic blend of cultural influences, with recipes ranging from those with Mediterranean flavors to variations of Ashkenazic-style traditional dishes.

Instead of the customary chicken broth for the matzo ball soup, basil-laced matzo balls float in a bright green spinach soup. I've included a baked fish loaf studded with asparagus and flavored with Moroccan herbs and spices in place of the more customary gefilte fish, an Eastern European dish of fish quenelles known to inspire either devotion or hatred. Quinoa, one of the few acceptable grains to eat during Passover, is baked into a kugel, or casserole, with sweet potatoes and prunes for a hearty vegetarian entrée. The chicken is braised in pomegranate molasses and sprinkled with walnuts. A potato and cauliflower smash is subtly spiced with saffron and caramelized leeks, and the chocolate almond brownies are sweetened with dates.

Along with the ritual feast, a seder plate holds a number of traditional symbolic foods, including a roasted lamb shank bone, a roasted egg, parsley, and horseradish or bitter greens.

One bowl is filled with haroset, a sweet mix of fruit and nuts that represents the mortar that held together the bricks the slaves in Egypt labored over. The mixture is ritually served during the seder on a piece of matzo topped with a slice of fresh horseradish, a sinus-clearing but tasty combination.

Ashkenazic-style haroset is best made within a couple of hours of the start of the seder. Mix ¾ cup lightly toasted pecans or walnuts or a combination of the two, 1 teaspoon ground cinnamon, 2 peeled and cored apples, and ⅓ cup sweet wine. Pulse in a food processor until well combined. Taste and add a teaspoon of sugar if necessary. Place in a bowl on the seder plate.

Cook's Notes

2 days in advance:

Make the fish terrine.
Make the brownies.
Make the eggplant salad.
Make the cauliflower-potato smash.

1 day in advance:

Make the chicken.

Make the spinach soup.

Make the Tzimmes Kugel.

Make the beet salad.

Day of:

Make the matzo balls.

Make the haroset (see page 193).

Make the spiced cilantro dressing for the fish terrine.

Reheat the chicken, cauliflower-potato smash, kugel, and soup.

Creamy Spinach Soup with Basil Matzo Balls

ALTHOUGH MATZO BALL SOUP is usually based in a chicken broth, you'll find this gorgeously green version quite refreshing. The soup is garlicky and rich and the herbed matzo ball rises out of the green broth like a hill against a green meadow.

SERVES 4 TO 6

2 tablespoons extra virgin olive oil

3 cups leeks, white and light green parts only, cut into small dice

2 celery stalks, cut into small dice

1 head garlic, cloves peeled and left whole

6 fresh thyme sprigs

1 medium (¼ pound) thin-skinned potato, peeled and cut into 1-inch chunks

5 cups water or vegetable stock (page 4 or 6)

Bay leaf

Salt

1½ pounds spinach, well washed, stems removed, leaves roughly chopped

1 cup fresh basil leaves

1 tablespoon fresh lemon juice

Freshly ground black pepper

1 recipe Basil Matzo Balls (page 196)

Warm the olive oil in a medium pot. Add the leeks and celery and sauté over medium heat 5 to 7 minutes, until softened. Add the garlic, thyme, potato, water, and bay leaf. Cover and bring to a boil. Add 1½ teaspoons salt, lower the heat, and simmer 20 to 25 minutes, until the garlic is tender. Remove and discard the thyme stems (most of the leaves will have fallen into the soup) and bay leaf.

Turn off the heat, stir in the spinach and basil, and let the heat of the soup wilt the spinach. It looks like a lot, but turn it with tongs and it will wilt down in about 3 minutes.

Blend the soup in batches until smooth. Return to the pot, stir in the lemon juice, and sprinkle with black pepper. Taste and add more salt if necessary.

Serve hot, with Basil Matzo Balls, or chilled.

Basil Matzo Balls

These extra light and fluffy matzo balls are a variation on the classic recipe from the Streits Matzo Meal package. Wisps of basil make these really pretty and give them great flavor.

MAKES 10 LARGE MATZO BALLS

4 eggs
¼ cup oil (see Note)
¼ cup sparkling water
1 teaspoon salt
Freshly ground black pepper
1 cup matzo meal
½ cup chopped fresh basil

Whisk the eggs in a medium bowl with the oil, sparkling water, salt, and a sprinkling of black pepper. Stir in the matzo meal and basil and combine thoroughly.

Refrigerate for at least 30 minutes.

Fill a large pot halfway with water and bring to a boil. With moistened hands, divide the batter into 10 balls. Drop them into the water and cover. Lower the heat and simmer until the balls are cooked through, about 30 minutes. Remove with a slotted spoon to a large bowl. Simmer in the soup before serving.

Note: Although you can use a variety of oils with the exception of olive oil, my favorite is melted coconut oil (expeller pressed with no coconut flavor, *not* extra virgin) or good old chicken fat for a really light and delicious matzo ball. If those don't appeal to you, use canola oil.

Fish Terrine with Asparagus and Ginger and Spiced Cilantro Dressing

GEFILTE FISH is an Ashkenazic tradition that people either love or revile. In this easy variation, the fish is flavored with ginger and herbs and baked with asparagus spears. When sliced, pieces of asparagus stud the loaf. This dish must be served chilled and can be made up to three days in advance. Have your fishmonger clean and grind the fish.

SERVES 10 TO 12 AS AN APPETIZER

8 asparagus stalks, preferably thick ones (about ½ pound), bottom 1½ inches trimmed

2 tablespoons extra virgin olive oil

2 cups minced onions

3 eggs

¼ cup matzo meal

¼ cup minced fresh ginger

¾ cup vegetable stock (page 4 or 6), chicken stock (page 5), or water

1½ pounds ground whitefish (about 4 pounds whole whitefish)

2 teaspoons salt

Freshly ground black pepper

¼ cup chopped fresh parsley

¼ cup chopped fresh cilantro

Juice of ½ lemon

Spiced Cilantro Dressing

1 cup finely chopped fresh cilantro

2 garlic cloves, minced

½ teaspoon salt

Large pinch of cayenne pepper

2 tablespoons fresh lemon juice

¼ cup extra virgin olive oil

2 teaspoons ground cumin

(continued)

MAKE THE TERRINE: Blanch the asparagus in a pot of boiling salted water until tender, about 3 minutes. Refresh with cold water and set aside.

Warm the olive oil in a medium skillet over medium heat. Add the onions and sauté until softened, about 10 minutes. Set aside to cool.

Preheat the oven to 350°F. Line a 9 x 5 x 2½-inch loaf pan with parchment paper, letting the paper overlap the long sides of the pan to create handles. Oil the two short sides of the pan where the parchment is not touching.

In a stand mixer fitted with a paddle or by hand, beat the eggs with the matzo meal until completely smooth, 2 to 3 minutes. Add the ginger, stock, fish, salt, a sprinkling of black pepper, the parsley, cilantro, and onions. Beat just until well combined, about 1 minute.

Ladle about ¾ inch of the mixture onto the bottom of the pan. Press 4 asparagus spears lengthwise into the terrine, alternating tips and feet, spacing them evenly. Ladle another ¾ inch of mixture over the asparagus, then arrange the next 4 asparagus. Top with the remaining fish mixture. Slam the pan on the countertop to eliminate any air bubbles. Squeeze the lemon juice over the top.

Place the loaf pan on a baking sheet (in case any drips over) and bake until a skewer inserted into the center comes out clean, 50 to 60 minutes.

MAKE THE DRESSING: Mix together the cilantro, garlic, salt, cayenne, and lemon juice in a small bowl.

Warm the oil and cumin in a small skillet over medium-low heat until the cumin smells fragrant, about 2 minutes. Stir into the cilantro mixture and thoroughly mix to combine.

Remove the terrine from the oven and cool. Wrap and refrigerate overnight. The terrine will firm as it cools. Invert the terrine and peel off the parchment paper. Cut into slices and serve with the cilantro dressing.

The terrine and dressing keep very well refrigerated for 3 to 4 days.

Pomegranate Chicken with Walnuts

POMEGRANATE MOLASSES, also known as pomegranate syrup, is an important ingredient in Turkish, Moroccan, and Persian cooking. Chicken is sautéed, then braised in the tart syrup, which turns into a beautiful mahogany glaze. Make this in advance and reheat it in a covered casserole at 350°F just until heated through.

If you double the recipe, cook it in an extra large skillet. There is no need to double the liquid. If you make this for times other than Passover, you can use unbleached white flour instead of matzo meal.

SERVES 4

I whole chicken, cut into parts (4 breasts, 2 legs, 2 thighs) or 4 legs and thighs
Salt and freshly ground black pepper
1/2 cup matzo meal
2 tablespoons extra virgin olive oil
3/4 cup water
2 cups thinly sliced onions
I cup pomegranate molasses
6 tablespoons sugar, preferably evaporated cane sugar or maple sugar
3/4 cup walnuts, lightly toasted and coarsely chopped
1/4 cup chopped parsley

Prepare the chicken by trimming any hanging fat. Salt and pepper the chicken parts. Spread the matzo meal on a plate and dredge the chicken on both sides.

Warm the olive oil in a large skillet over medium-high heat. Add the chicken, skin side down, and sauté until well browned, about 6 minutes on the first side, 3 to 4 on the second. Turn off the heat, remove the chicken from the skillet, place in a bowl, and set aside.

Pour off all but a thin film of fat from the skillet. Add 1/4 cup of the water and scrape up any brown bits. Add the onions and sauté over medium heat until softened, about 5 minutes. Stir in the molasses, the remaining 1/2 cup water, the sugar, and 1/2 teaspoon salt. Return the chicken to the skillet along with any pan juices and spoon some liquid over the chicken. Bring the liquid to a boil, cover, and lower the heat to a gentle simmer. Braise for

(continued)

25 to 40 minutes, turning the chicken every 10 minutes, just until the chicken is fork-tender. Remove the pieces to a plate as they get tender so they do not overcook. Rapidly simmer the liquid in the skillet, uncovered, until reduced and thickened, about 5 to 10 minutes. Return the chicken to the skillet and baste with the sauce.

Serve, topped with the walnuts and sprinkled with parsley.

Tzimmes Kugel

SWEET POTATOES and prunes often appear together in an Ashkenazic dish called tzimmes. Here they are baked into a flavorful casserole of quinoa laced with caramelized onions and cinnamon. This high-protein dish makes a luscious accompaniment to the rest of the meal, or it can be served as a vegetarian entrée.

SERVES 6 TO 8

¾ cup quinoa
1½ cups water
Salt
1 pound sweet potatoes, peeled and thinly sliced into ⅛-inch rounds
½ cup packed, pitted prunes, quartered (4 ounces)
¼ cup extra virgin olive oil
3 cups thinly sliced onions (3 medium)
4 eggs
Freshly ground black pepper
1 teaspoon ground cinnamon
½ teaspoon orange zest
½ cup chopped fresh dill

Rinse the quinoa in a strainer and dry-toast it in a small pot over medium-high heat until almost dry. Add the water and a pinch of salt. Cover and bring to a boil. Lower the heat to a simmer and cook, covered, until the grains have swelled and the water is absorbed, about 15 minutes. Do not disturb the steam vents that will form while the quinoa is cooking. Remove the pot from the heat and pour the quinoa into a large bowl.

Meanwhile, steam the sweet potatoes for about 8 minutes, until very tender. Add to the quinoa along with the prunes.

Preheat the oven to 350°F. Warm 2 tablespoons of the oil in a large skillet. Add the onions and sauté over medium-high heat until the onions are browned, about 10 minutes. Add the onions to the quinoa mixture. In a small bowl, whisk together the eggs, 1 1/2 teaspoons salt, a generous sprinkling of black pepper, the cinnamon, and orange zest. Add to the quinoa mixture along with the dill. Gently stir to combine thoroughly.

Pour 1 tablespoon of the oil into a 9-inch ovenproof pie plate (Pyrex is preferable) and place it in the oven for a couple of minutes until the oil is hot. Remove the pan, swirl the oil around to coat the bottom of the pan, and pour the quinoa mixture into the pan, evening it out with a spatula. Return to the oven and bake, uncovered, for 30 minutes. Remove the kugel and drizzle the remaining 1 tablespoon oil over the top. Put the dish back in the oven and bake for 20 to 30 minutes longer, until golden brown.

Unmold the kugel by loosening the edges with a knife and sliding it onto a serving platter. Serve hot or at room temperature.

Potato-Cauliflower Smash with Caramelized Leeks and Saffron

CAULIFLOWER AND POTATOES are browned, braised, and mashed with golden leeks in this light, yet rich and comforting dish. The saffron lends an exotic Mediterranean taste and delicate lemon color.

SERVES 6 TO 8

¼ cup extra virgin olive oil
1½ pounds Yukon gold potatoes, peeled and cut into ¾-inch cubes (4 cups)
4 cups cauliflower florets (from a 1¼- to 1½-pound cauliflower)
1½ teaspoons salt
Freshly ground black pepper
1½ cups water
1 tablespoon fresh lemon juice
2 cups leeks, white and light green parts only, quartered and cut into ¼-inch pieces
Large pinch of saffron threads, dissolved in 2 tablespoons boiling water

Warm 2 tablespoons of the olive oil in a large skillet over medium heat until shimmering. Add the potatoes, cauliflower, salt, and a generous sprinkling of black pepper. Sauté the vegetables, turning several times, until they are browned in places (they won't be browned on all sides), being careful not to burn them. You may have a lot of brown bits sticking to the pan at this point; just make sure they are not blackened. Add the water to the pan and deglaze by scraping up the flavorful brown bits.

Cover and simmer until the vegetables are completely tender, about 15 minutes. Uncover and mash the vegetables, stirring to soak up the pan juices. Stir in the lemon juice.

Meanwhile, warm the remaining 2 tablespoons oil over medium heat in a medium skillet. Add the leeks and sauté until caramelized, about 5 minutes. Stir the leeks, saffron, and any remaining oil into the potatoes, and stir well to combine.

Taste and add additional salt, pepper, and an extra splash of lemon juice if desired. Serve hot.

This can be made in advance and reheated in a covered casserole in a preheated 350°F oven.

Moroccan Eggplant Salad

SALTING THE EGGPLANT for this North African–inspired eggplant salad takes away any bitterness, and roasting the eggplant softens it beautifully without making it too oily.

Although eggplants are not in the height of season at this time of year, these Mediterranean staples are traditional in Sephardic seders the world over. The smaller Italian eggplants are readily available and surprisingly flavorful.

MAKES 3 CUPS (SERVES 6)

2 pounds eggplant, preferably several medium-small ones
Salt
1/4 cup extra virgin olive oil
3 garlic cloves, minced
1 teaspoon paprika
1 teaspoon ground cumin
1/4 teaspoon cayenne pepper
2 tablespoons fresh lemon juice
2 tablespoons chopped fresh parsley
2 tablespoons chopped fresh cilantro
Freshly ground black pepper

Peel the eggplant lengthwise, leaving alternating 1/2-inch stripes of peel. Cut the eggplant crosswise into 1/4-inch rounds. Place in a bowl and add 1 teaspoon of salt to the eggplant and toss to combine. Place in a colander or leave in the bowl for at least 30 minutes to sweat.

Preheat the oven to 375°F.

With paper towels, wipe down the eggplant and place in a medium bowl. Toss with 2 tablespoons of the oil and place on parchment-covered baking sheets. Roast until the eggplant is tender, about 30 minutes. Remove from the oven and let cool.

Chop the eggplant into 1/2-inch pieces. Place in a medium bowl and stir in the garlic, paprika, cumin, and cayenne.

Warm the remaining 2 tablespoons of oil over medium heat in a large nonstick skillet. Add the eggplant mixture and cook, stirring from time to time, for about 5 minutes, until the spices are heated through. Return the eggplant to the bowl and stir in the lemon juice, parsley, cilantro, and a sprinkling of black pepper. Taste and add additional salt if necessary.

Beet Salad with Apple and Celery

BEETS TINT the apple a beautiful rose, and the celery provides a contrasting crunch. This is a great make-ahead dish.

MAKES 5 CUPS (SERVES 6)

1 pound beets, preferably small
1 Granny Smith apple, cored, peeled, quartered, and thinly sliced
2 tablespoons minced shallot
2 celery stalks, thinly sliced on the diagonal
2 tablespoons chopped fresh dill
1 tablespoon fresh lemon juice
1 tablespoon balsamic vinegar
1 tablespoon walnut oil or extra virgin olive oil
1/4 teaspoon salt
Freshly ground black pepper

In a medium pot, cover the beets with water and bring to a boil. Lower the heat and simmer until the beets are tender, about 1 hour or so, depending on the size. Alternatively, put the beets in a pressure cooker with just enough water to cover. Bring the water to a boil, lock the lid into pressure, and cook for 15 minutes, until tender. Release the lid using the quick-release method. Check to see that the beets are tender.

Remove the beets from the water, slip the skins off, and cut into 1/4-inch wedges. Place in a medium bowl. You should have 3 cups.

Add the apple, shallot, celery, and dill. Stir in the lemon juice, vinegar, oil, and salt. Sprinkle with black pepper. Let sit for at least 20 minutes to allow the flavors to marry.

Fudge Brownies with Almonds and Dates

*T*HESE BROWNIES stay moist for days, slice beautifully, and are deliciously rich and choc-olaty but not heavy. If you have no objection to butter, use it for the most delectable flavor. Accompany these brownies with raspberry sorbet.

MAKES 36 SMALL BROWNIES

1½ cups dates, pitted
1 cup whole almonds, toasted (see Note)
¼ cup cocoa powder
½ teaspoon ground cinnamon
1 teaspoon vanilla extract
Pinch of salt
6 ounces semisweet chocolate, cut into small pieces
4 tablespoons (½ stick) unsalted butter (optional)
3 eggs, lightly beaten

Preheat the oven to 325°F. Line an 8 x 8-inch baking pan with parchment paper or foil, letting the paper overlap the pan to create handles. Oil the two sides where the parchment is not touching.

Place the dates in a small pot with water to cover. Bring the liquid to a boil and turn off. Let the dates soften for 10 minutes.

Meanwhile, process the almonds in a food processor until they are the consistency of flour. Transfer to a medium bowl.

Drain the dates, reserving ¼ cup of the soaking liquid. Process the dates until smooth, using some or all of the soaking liquid to make a smooth purée. Add the purée to the al-monds along with the cocoa, cinnamon, vanilla, and salt.

Melt the chocolate and butter, if using, in a double boiler over simmering water. Stir the chocolate and eggs into the batter and mix well.

Pour into the prepared baking pan, smooth evenly, and bake for 25 to 30 minutes. A toothpick in the middle should come out moist. Do not overbake. Remove from the oven and let cool for at least 30 minutes. Lift the whole brownie out of the pan and

(continued)

cut into squares. Store at room temperature for up to a week or freeze for up to 2 months.

Note: To toast the nuts, place them on a baking sheet and toast in a preheated 350°F oven for 10 minutes. Let cool before grinding. If you prefer, you can use packaged almond flour instead, which will have a milder flavor. You will need 1 cup.

- Sesame-Crusted Haloumi Cheese with Olive-Mint Gremolata 211

- Chickpea Cakes with Red Pepper Skordalia 212

- Hortopita 214

- Halibut with Pine Nuts, Saffron, and Currants 216

- Thyme-Braised Artichokes with Mushrooms and Peas 217

- Oregano-Roasted Potato Fans with Cucumber, Dill, and Yogurt Dip 218

- Baklava Cups with Almond-Vanilla Tapioca Pudding and Strawberry-Rhubarb Compote 220

ONSIDERED THE MOST joyous holiday on the Christian calendar, Easter cele-brates the resurrection of Jesus Christ. Traditionally, Easter is a time of mira-cles, or reaffirmation of faith. Sunrise services and baptisms are commonly held outside on Easter morning, and a large meal is eaten later in the day. In the West, Easter falls on the first Sunday following the full moon that occurs on or following the spring equinox, a time to shed heavy clothing and don bright colors. Easter is a movable feast since it falls anywhere between March 22 and April 25. The Eastern Orthodox Christian churches use the older tables based on the Julian calendar, and the holiday usually falls a week or so later. The name "Easter" most likely comes from the Scandinavian *Ostra* or Teu-tonic *Ostern* or *Eastere,* the Anglo-Saxon goddess of spring to whom the month of April was dedicated.

The Lenten season, which includes the forty-six days (excluding Sundays) before Easter, is the period of penitence in preparation for the bright holiday that follows the season of grief. Traditionally, it is a period of abstaining from specific foods, and of almsgiving and prayer. Nowadays, people often give up one indulgence or bad habit. The Lenten season concludes with Holy Week, the last week of Lent, which includes Palm Sunday, the day Je-sus entered Jerusalem. Holy Thursday before Easter recalls the Last Supper; Friday, the Cru-cifixion; and Sunday, the Resurrection.

Eggs, a symbol of fertility and new life, were traditionally forbidden during Lent. On Easter, eggs are celebrated; they are consumed, dyed, decorated, given as gifts, and used for egg-rolling games. Rolling decorated Easter eggs is seen to represent the rolling away of the rock from the tomb of Jesus. In the United States there's an annual Easter egg roll on the White House lawn. Ukrainians in particular are known for their elaborate Easter egg de-signs. Egg colors vary by country; gold and silver are favored by Slavic peoples, red in Greece, and green in parts of Germany and Austria.

Although in America foods for Easter are as various as people's diverse heritages, I'm drawn to the flavors of Greece. In the Greek tradition, Easter is the most important holiday of the year. Although this menu features fish and vegetarian fare, should you wish to include a traditional roast leg of lamb, it would be compatible with the rest of these dishes. Appetizers include savory mini chickpea cakes topped with zesty red pepper skordalia and Sesame-Crusted Haloumi Cheese with Olive-Mint Gremolata. The centerpiece of the meal is a Hortopita, a crustless greens pie, with chicory, romaine, feta cheese, herbs, eggs, and cornmeal baked into a light cakelike quiche. The halibut is braised with fennel and saffron and enhanced with pine nuts and currants. A baby artichoke, mushroom, and pea braise accompanies these mains along with oregano-roasted "fanned" potatoes that are topped with a thick and luscious garlicky cucumber, yogurt, and dill dip. The dramatic dessert includes individual pistachio phyllo cups topped with a strawberry-rhubarb compote draped over a honey-laced tapioca pudding. Every bite is a medley of wonderful flavors and diverse textures. Enjoy this Greek-style feast at Easter or throughout the spring season.

Cook's Notes

1 week in advance:

Make the baklava phyllo cups and store at room temperature.

2 days in advance:

Make the Red Pepper Skordalia.
Make the Strawberry-Rhubarb Compote.
Drain the yogurt for the Cucumber, Dill, and Yogurt Dip.
Roast the garlic for the dip.

Day before:

Finish the yogurt dip.
Make the tapioca pudding.
Form the chickpea patties.

Make the Hortopita.

Coat the haloumi cheese in sesame seeds and make the olive topping.

Day of:

Sauté the chickpea patties; rewarm before serving.

Bake the potato fans; rewarm before serving.

Sauté the onions and fennel for the fish.

Prepare the vegetables except for the peas.

Right before serving:

Add the fish and finish cooking.

Add the peas to the vegetables and warm.

Sauté the haloumi cheese.

Sesame-Crusted Haloumi Cheese with Olive-Mint Gremolata

*H*ALOUMI IS a delicious cheese from Cyprus that can be sautéed or grilled. Dredged in sesame seeds, this appetizer cooks to a golden brown and is sprinkled with gremolata, a zesty olive-mint-garlic-lemon topping.

Haloumi cheese is readily available in gourmet markets and Middle Eastern stores.

SERVES 6

⅓ cup finely chopped olives, preferably kalamata
1 tablespoon chopped fresh mint
½ teaspoon lemon zest
1 garlic clove, minced
½ pound haloumi cheese
6 tablespoons sesame seeds
Extra virgin olive oil, for sautéing

In a small bowl, stir together the olives, mint, zest, and garlic. Set aside.

Slice the cheese ¼ inch thick; you should have about 12 slices. Spread the sesame seeds on a plate. Dredge the cheese in the seeds, pressing firmly so that they adhere.

Film a large nonstick skillet with oil and warm over medium-high heat. Add the cheese and sauté until golden brown, about 2 minutes per side. Serve warm, with a dollop of gremolata on each slice.

chickpea cakes with Red Pepper skordalia

*T*HESE PRETTY little patties are flecked with dill and served with a zesty topping. You can make them larger if you like and serve them as a vegan main course. For convenience, sauté the cakes a few hours early, then reheat them in a 350°F oven for 10 to 15 minutes.

MAKES TWELVE ¼-CUP PATTIES

¼ cup extra virgin olive oil, plus more for sautéing
1 cup minced onion
1 jalapeño pepper, preferably red, stemmed, seeded, and minced
2 garlic cloves, minced
½ cup thinly sliced scallions, white and green parts
3 cups cooked chickpeas (from two 15-ounce cans, drained, or 1½ cups dried)
¾ teaspoon salt
½ cup chopped fresh dill
2 teaspoons fresh lemon juice
Freshly ground black pepper
1 recipe Red Pepper Skordalia

Warm 2 tablespoons of the olive oil in a medium skillet. Add the onions and sauté over medium heat until softened and starting to brown, about 7 minutes. Add the jalapeño, garlic, and scallions, and cook an additional 2 minutes, until the scallions are softened.

Turn off the heat, but leave the vegetables in the skillet on the stove. Stir in the chickpeas, an additional 2 tablespoons of oil, and the salt, mashing to break up the chickpeas. You don't have to mash all of them completely, just enough so that you can easily form them into patties.

Transfer the mixture to a medium bowl until cool enough to handle. Stir in the dill and lemon juice and sprinkle with black pepper. Taste and add additional salt if necessary.

To form patties, use a ¼-cup measure, and pack tightly with the chickpea mixture. You should have 12 patties.

Lightly film a nonstick skillet with oil and warm over medium-high heat. Put in half the patties and sauté until golden, about 4 minutes per side. Repeat with the remaining patties. Alternatively, place the patties on an oiled parchment-covered baking sheet. Brush the tops with oil and bake in a 350°F oven until golden, about 20 minutes. Serve hot, topped with the skordalia.

Red Pepper Skordalia

Skordalia is a garlicky dip, usually made with potatoes or bread and almonds. In this variation, a roasted red pepper enriches the mix. It is also delicious on the Hortopita and the potato fans.

MAKES 1 CUP

1 roasted red pepper (½ cup jarred)
1 piece sourdough or country-style bread, 4 x 4 inches, ½ inch thick, crusts removed
6 tablespoons extra virgin olive oil
¼ cup blanched almonds
2 garlic cloves, crushed with ½ teaspoon salt
1 tablespoon fresh lemon juice
1 tablespoon red wine vinegar

Place all the ingredients in a blender and blend until smooth.

Hortopita

*H*ORTOPITA MEANS "greens pie" in Greek. In this festive version, chicory, romaine lettuce, and herbs are combined with feta cheese, cornmeal, and eggs and baked into a light crustless pie with a cakelike texture. The Hortopita can be made in advance. It also makes a delicious brunch dish. The cup or so of liquid left at the bottom of the pot after cooking the greens, called pot liquor, makes a revitalizing tonic.

MAKES ONE 8 X 8-INCH PIE (SERVES 6)

2 bunches chicory (1½ to 2 pounds), bottom 1½ inches of hard stems removed, cut
    into bite-sized pieces
1 head romaine, shredded
1 teaspoon salt
¼ cup extra virgin olive oil
2 cups well-washed leeks, white part only, chopped
½ cup thinly sliced scallions, white and green parts
½ cup chopped parsley
½ cup chopped sorrel (optional)
1 cup crumbled feta cheese, preferably Greek
1 cup grated kasseri cheese, other sheep's milk cheese, or Gruyère or aged goat cheese
¼ cup pitted kalamata olives, sliced into ¼-inch rings (12 olives)
½ cup cornmeal
½ teaspoon baking powder
4 eggs, lightly beaten
Freshly ground black pepper
2 tablespoons butter, coconut oil, or olive oil

Preheat the oven to 350°F. Have ready an 8 x 8-inch baking dish.

Wash the chicory and romaine; there is no need to dry them. Put the chicory and salt in a large pot and wilt it over medium heat, stirring frequently or tossing with tongs to push the uncooked leaves to the bottom of the pot. You don't have to add water to the pot because the water clinging to the leaves from washing is enough to cook them. Don't be daunted by the quantity of greens, as they reduce significantly when wilted. Cook until the leaves have wilted and shrunken, about 5 minutes. Add the romaine and toss frequently, another minute or two, until wilted. Remove and place in a strainer. Squeeze against the strainer to remove excess water. Place on a cutting board and chop into small pieces; you should have 4 cups of greens. Transfer to a large bowl.

Wipe out the pot. Pour in the oil and leeks and sauté over medium heat until the leeks are softened, about 5 minutes. Add the scallions and cook another 3 minutes or so. Add the scallions and leeks to the greens along with the parsley and sorrel, if using. Stir in the cheeses, olives, cornmeal, baking powder, eggs, and a sprinkling of black pepper and combine thoroughly.

Place 1 tablespoon of butter in the baking dish and place in the oven for 5 minutes or so, until hot. Remove from the oven and rotate the pan to make sure the melted butter covers the bottom of the baking dish. Immediately pour in the greens mixture and spread it evenly. Return to the oven and bake for 30 minutes. Remove from the oven and dot the remaining tablespoon of butter or drizzle the oil over the top. Return to the oven and bake an additional 30 minutes, until the top is golden brown. Remove from the oven and let cool for a few minutes. Cut into squares and serve hot or at room temperature.

Halibut with Pine Nuts, Saffron, and Currants

*H*ERE IS colorful stovetop dish, easy enough for a weeknight dinner.

SERVES 6

¼ cup pine nuts
¼ cup extra virgin olive oil
1 medium fennel bulb, cored and thinly sliced (1 cup), some fronds reserved for garnish
1 medium onion, thinly sliced (1 cup)
¼ cup tomato paste
½ cup water
Pinch of saffron
½ cup white wine
Salt
¼ cup currants
1½ pounds halibut fillets, skinned
Freshly ground black pepper

Dry-toast the pine nuts in a large heavy-bottomed skillet over medium heat until golden, about 4 minutes. Set the pine nuts aside.

Pour the olive oil into the same skillet. Add the fennel and onion and sauté over medium-low heat until the vegetables are tender and browned, about 15 minutes.

Meanwhile, combine the tomato paste and water in a small bowl with the saffron, wine, and 1 teaspoon salt. Add the liquid to the skillet. Bring to a boil, lower the heat, and simmer for about 3 minutes or so, uncovered, until the sauce is thickened. Stir in the currants and fish, and sprinkle the fish with salt and black pepper to taste.

Cover and cook 5 to 7 minutes, depending on the thickness. (It could even be a few minutes more if the fillets are over an inch thick.) Uncover and check to make sure there is enough liquid in the pan. Add a couple of tablespoons of water if necessary.

Serve hot, with the sauce spooned over the fish. Sprinkle with the reserved pine nuts and fennel fronds.

Thyme-Braised Artichokes with Mushrooms and Peas

THIS IS a beautiful medley of spring vegetables, simply braised with garlic and fresh thyme. Although expensive, morels are sublime in this dish, and a quarter pound goes a long way; you can substitute fresh shiitakes. For convenience, use frozen peas. Toss them in at the end; they cook in minutes.

SERVES 4

12 baby artichokes
Lemon juice
½ pound baby carrots
¼ cup extra virgin olive oil
Salt
10 fresh thyme sprigs
¼ pound fresh morels, halved, or ½ pound shiitake mushrooms, wiped clean, stemmed,
    and sliced
3 garlic cloves, minced
½ cup peas
Freshly ground black pepper

Before trimming the artichokes, have ready a bowl with acidulated water (3 tablespoons lemon juice to 1 quart water) to drop the artichokes into as they're trimmed. To trim the artichokes snap off the outer leaves by pulling them downward until they break off at the base. Keep pulling off the leaves until you get to the tender yellow leaves and only the top third are green. Slice off the top third green part. Trim off the dark green leaves with a vegetable peeler where the leaves were pulled off and also the green outer skin of the stem. Cut off the tippy end, but leave the stem intact. Smooth any rough areas around the base. Cut the artichokes in half and place the halves you're not working with in the acidulated water. No need to remove the choke—the baby ones are not developed.

Blanch the carrots in a small pot of salted boiling water until tender, about 4 to 5 minutes. Drain and reserve.

(continued)

In a large skillet, combine the artichokes, 2 tablespoons of the olive oil, 1/4 cup of water, 1/2 teaspoon salt, and the fresh thyme. Cover and cook over medium heat until the artichokes are just tender, about 7 minutes.

Meanwhile, rinse the morels briefly. Warm the remaining 2 tablespoons oil in a medium skillet over medium-high heat. Add the mushrooms and a sprinkling of salt and sauté for 2 to 3 minutes. Add the garlic and sauté until golden, about 3 to 4 minutes. When the artichokes are tender, uncover them and add the mushrooms to the artichokes along with the carrots and peas. You can cook the dish to this point up to an hour in advance. Sauté all of the vegetables together until the peas are tender and all the vegetables are heated through. Sprinkle with a bit more salt, a generous sprinkling of black pepper, and a squeeze of lemon juice. Serve hot. Leave in the thyme sprigs, since they look pretty on the plate.

Note: You can save the shiitake stems and add them to the stockpot. They're too tough to eat, but they add a wonderful flavor.

Oregano-Roasted Potato Fans with Cucumber, Dill, and Yogurt Dip

POTATOES ROASTED with oregano are traditional in Greek cooking. In this easy and elegant dish, individual potatoes are thinly sliced but left whole. They are roasted with herbs tucked between the slices and become crispy after an hour in the oven. The thick garlicky yogurt dip with cucumber is a creamy and crunchy accompaniment.

Scale up the number of potatoes to include as many as you need. This does not take long to prepare if you roast a head of garlic and drain the yogurt the night before you need it. Thick Greek-style yogurt, now widely available, does not need to be drained, so you'll need only 1 cup.

MAKES 1 1/2 CUPS DIP (SERVES 4)

Dip

 2 cups plain yogurt

 1 small head garlic, roasted (see page 10)

 ¼ teaspoon salt

 1 cup finely chopped parsley

 ¼ cup chopped fresh dill

 ½ teaspoon Dijon mustard

 ½ medium cucumber, peeled and seeded, cut into small dice (about ½ cup)

Potatoes

 4 medium thin-skinned potatoes (½ pound each)

 2 tablespoons extra virgin olive oil

 1½ teaspoons salt

 2 teaspoons dried oregano

MAKE THE DIP: Pour the yogurt into a strainer lined with a double layer of cheesecloth over a medium bowl. Let drain for at least an hour in the refrigerator and up to overnight. The yogurt will have thickened considerably and you'll have about 1 cup.

Squeeze out the cloves from the roasted garlic, mash them, and set aside in a small bowl.

Add the yogurt to the garlic along with the salt, parsley, dill, mustard, and cucumber. Stir just until combined.

PREPARE THE POTATOES: Preheat the oven to 400°F.

Insert a metal or wooden skewer through each potato about ½ inch from the bottom on the long side. Slice off a ⅛- to ¼-inch slab of the potato so the potato can lie flat on the cutting board. Slice the potato thinly, cuts about ⅛ inch apart, cutting as far down as the skewer. Remove the skewer after you have finished slicing.

Have ready a ramekin with the oil and a pastry brush. Place the potatoes on a parchment-covered baking sheet. Pry the slices gently open with your fingers as you brush a little oil on each slice.

Mix together the salt and oregano in a small cup. Sprinkle each potato with the salt, pushing the slices gently apart with your fingers to season between the slices.

Place in the oven and roast, uncovered, until the potatoes are tender and the slices are crisp, about 70 to 80 minutes. Remove from the oven and serve hot.

Baklava Cups with Almond-Vanilla Tapioca Pudding and Strawberry-Rhubarb Compote

*T*HIS DESSERT appears to be complicated, but it is actually quite simple, especially since all three parts can be made in advance. Flowerlike phyllo cups hold a lightly sweetened tapioca pudding made with almond milk and mixed with a swirl of honey. A rosy strawberry rhubarb compote is spooned over the tapioca. Spiced pistachios, nestled between the layers of phyllo, are a delicious and chewy surprise.

The cups can be made up to a week in advance and stored at room temperature. Rose water is available in gourmet markets, natural foods stores, and any store selling Middle Eastern products.

SERVES 12

Phyllo Cups

1 cup shelled pistachios or walnuts, or a mixture

¼ teaspoon ground cinnamon

Pinch of ground cloves

2 tablespoons rice syrup

2 tablespoons maple sugar or unrefined cane sugar

1 teaspoon rose water

8 sheets phyllo dough, defrosted

Coconut oil, melted, or butter, melted

Tapioca

½ cup instant or minute tapioca

3 cups fresh almond milk (page 222)

Salt

1 vanilla bean

2 eggs, lightly beaten

¼ cup sugar, preferably maple or granulated cane sugar

1 teaspoon grated lemon zest

½ teaspoon rose water

2 tablespoons honey

Strawberry-Rhubarb Compote

   3 rhubarb stalks (about ¾ pound), cut into ½-inch pieces (3 cups)

   ½ cup plus 2 tablespoons sugar, preferably maple or evaporated cane juice

   ½ teaspoon rose water

   2 cups hulled and quartered strawberries

   Grated zest of 1 lemon

MAKE THE PHYLLO CUPS: Preheat the oven to 375°F.

Chop the pistachios and mix them in a small bowl with the cinnamon, cloves, rice syrup, maple sugar, and rose water until well combined.

Spread out the phyllo dough, making sure to keep covered what is not being used. Place a sheet of phyllo on a clean surface and lightly brush on a layer of coconut oil or melted butter, making sure to cover the entire exposed surface. Do this with a light touch. Add another sheet of phyllo on top of the first and brush with more oil or melted butter.

Cut the phyllo in half lengthwise. Cut each half into thirds. You should have 6 squares. If necessary, trim the squares with a knife to even them out.

Press each square into a muffin tin, folding and ruffling the phyllo until you get a desirable shape. (See illustrations below.) You should have a flowerlike holder. Repeat, placing

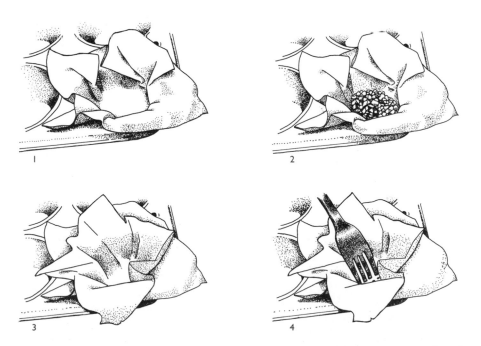

(continued)

the phyllo into every other cup. In a muffin pan for 12 muffins, you should be able to fit 6 phyllo cups. Place a tablespoon of the nuts in the bottom of each cup.

Prepare another 2 layers of phyllo so you have 6 more squares. Fit a second square on top of each holder, covering the nuts and ruffling the edges so that they look like flowers.

Poke holes in the bottom with a fork or a paring knife to keep the phyllo from puffing up during baking. Every cup will have its own character, depending on how you ruffle and fold the edges.

Bake the phyllo about 6 to 8 minutes, or until golden brown. Remove and continue with the remainder. Store at room temperature for up to a week in a covered container.

MAKE THE TAPIOCA: Mix the tapioca, almond milk, and a pinch of salt in a medium pot. Split open the vanilla bean, scrape out the seeds with the tip of a knife, and add the seeds to the almond milk. Reserve the pod for the fruit. Bring to a boil, lower the heat, and cook at a gentle simmer for 2 minutes.

Whisk together the eggs and sugar in a medium bowl. Slowly add the hot tapioca mixture to the beaten eggs, whisking constantly to raise their temperature and to avoid curdling.

Return the mixture to the saucepan and continue to cook on low heat for 3 to 6 minutes, stirring constantly, until noticeably thickened. Remove from the heat and stir in the lemon zest and rose water. Pour into a shallow pan and cool. Refrigerate, covered, until chilled. Fold the honey into the tapioca, distributing it throughout the pudding but letting streaks remain.

MAKE THE STRAWBERRY-RHUBARB COMPOTE: Preheat the oven to 350°F. Toss the rhubarb in a bowl with 1/2 cup of the sugar, the reserved vanilla pod, and rose water. Transfer to a baking dish, cover, and bake 20 minutes, until the rhubarb is almost tender. Scrape the pod to get any remaining seeds off, add them to the rhubarb, and bake an additional 10 minutes. Remove from the oven and allow to cool.

Meanwhile, toss the strawberries with the remaining 2 tablespoons sugar and the lemon zest in a bowl. Stir the rhubarb into the strawberries and let them macerate for 30 minutes. To serve, spoon 1/4 cup tapioca into each phyllo cup, then top with a heaping tablespoon of compote.

Almond Milk

In a blender, blend 1 cup blanched almonds and 3 cups water together until smooth. Pour through a cheesecloth-lined strainer, squeezing the cheesecloth to extract as much liquid as possible. You should have 3 cups. If you measure a little under 3 cups, add water to make up the difference.

Cinco de Mayo

- *Tortilla Soup* **226**

- *Strawberry Guacamole with Jícama Chips* **227**

- *Asparagus Quesadillas with Red Chile Paste* **229**

- *Smoky Caesar Salad with Manchego and Pine Nuts* **230**

- *Black Bean and Plantain—Stuffed Peppers* **231**

- *Coconut-Cornmeal—Crusted Tilapia with Tomatillo-Pumpkin Mole* **232**

- *Coconut Crème Caramel with Roasted Banana—Chocolate Sauce* **234**

INCO DE MAYO commemorates the victory of poorly armed Mexican troops led by General Ignacio Zaragoza over the well-outfitted occupying French forces in the Battle of Puebla on May 5, 1862. Although the Mexicans won the battle but lost the war, the improbable victory at the Battle of Puebla helped to develop a much-needed sense of national pride and unity. The holiday is not to be confused with Mexican Independence Day, which occurred nearly fifty years before, on September 16, 1810.

In Mexico, Cinco de Mayo is observed mostly as a regional holiday in Puebla, but it is widely observed in the United States by people of all ethnic origins, especially in parts of the country that have a high population of people with Mexican heritage. Zaragoza himself was born in Texas when it was still part of Mexico and is widely regarded as a Chicano hero. Cinco de Mayo is a joyful holiday celebrated with parades, mariachi music, *folklorico* dancing, and lots of feasting. More and more people each year take part in the party celebrating Mexican culture, music, and food.

The Mexican feast presents unexpected twists and exciting variations on some familiar dishes. Guacamole is studded with sweet strawberries. Make the basic chile paste a week in advance, if you like, since it keeps a long while; it gives an unexpected and *picante* flavor to the asparagus quesadillas. Tortilla soup here is endlessly adaptable to suit your preference. A variation on the traditional Caesar salad, truly a Mexican dish invented in Tijuana, is included here in a variation with lime juice, manchego cheese, and pine nuts with a touch of smoky paprika. For the main course, there are fat red peppers stuffed with refried black beans and ripe plantains, and tilapia crusted with cornmeal and coconut, both served on a pool of tomatillo–pumpkinseed sauce. Finish the meal with an easy-to-make Coconut Crème Caramel with Roasted Banana–Chocolate Sauce, and you'll have yourself quite a fiesta.

Cook's Notes

Up to a month before:

Make the chile paste.

Week before:

Make the vegetable or chicken stock for the soup.

2 days before:

Make the soup (without garnish).
Make the Caesar dressing.
Make the Coconut Crème Caramel with Roasted Banana–Chocolate Sauce.

Day before:

Make the stuffed peppers.
Make the tomatillo sauce.

Day of:

Wash the greens for the salad.
Make the soup garnishes.
Make the quesadillas.
Sauté the fish.
Make the guacamole.
Rewarm the Roasted Banana–Chocolate Sauce.

Tortilla Soup

THE CRISPY tortillas stick out of the broth like sails on a boat. Since the soup relies on a good stock, this is the place to make a good homemade vegetarian or chicken one.

SERVES 6

2 tablespoons extra virgin olive oil
1 cup diced onion
2 garlic cloves, minced
2 dried pasilla chiles, stemmed, seeded, and chopped into pieces
One 14-ounce can whole tomatoes, drained
6 cups chicken stock, All-Purpose Vegetable Stock, or Roasted Root Vegetable Stock
    (pages 5, 6, or 4)
1 cup fresh or frozen corn kernels (optional)
1 tablespoon fresh lime juice
Salt

Garnish
4 teaspoons extra virgin olive oil
4 corn tortillas, cut into strips
Salt
¼ cup chopped fresh cilantro
½ cup Cheddar or Jack cheese, preferably raw, cut into medium dice, or queso fresco
Sliced avocado
Shredded cooked chicken (optional)

Warm the oil in a medium pot or saucepan. Add the onion, garlic, and chiles, and cook over medium-low heat until the onion and garlic soften and start to brown, about 10 minutes. Transfer to a blender, add the tomatoes, and purée. Flecks of chiles will still remain.

Return the mixture to the pot and simmer the purée for 10 minutes, until reduced by half. Stir in the stock, cover, and bring to a boil. Lower the heat and simmer for 30 minutes, partially covered. Stir in the corn kernels the last 5 minutes, if using. Stir in the lime juice and sprinkle with salt to taste.

MAKE THE GARNISH: Have a paper towel–lined plate ready. Warm the oil in a large nonstick skillet. Add all the tortilla strips and toss and cook over medium-high heat until crispy and lightly golden, about 3 to 5 minutes. Transfer to the paper towel–lined plate and sprinkle with salt.

Serve the soup hot, garnishing each serving with a sprinkling of cilantro, a few cheese cubes, some avocado slices, the chicken, if using, and the tortilla strips.

Strawberry Guacamole with Jicama Chips

STRAWBERRIES, WHICH GO surprisingly well with avocados, add a sweet, succulent note to this festive guacamole. For the prettiest look, make sure to save some to garnish the top.

SERVES 6

2 ripe avocados

2 tablespoons fresh lime juice

1 teaspoon salt

2 scallions, white and green parts, thinly sliced on the diagonal

2 fresh serrano chiles, stemmed, seeded, and minced

¼ cup chopped cilantro

1 cup strawberries, rinsed, hulled, and sliced, plus a few sliced strawberries
   for garnish

1 pound jícama

Scoop the avocado flesh into a medium bowl and mash with a fork. Stir in the lime juice, salt, scallions, chiles, and cilantro, and combine well. Gently stir in the strawberries and sprinkle some on top for garnish.

Peel and cut the jícama into thin slices. Serve the guacamole surrounded with the jícama.

Asparagus Quesadillas with Red Chile Paste

THESE WHOLE grain quesadillas are spread with a thin layer of Red Chile Paste and stuffed with sliced asparagus. With the chile paste already prepared, making these takes just minutes. A dollop of guacamole on top would provide just the right sweet and cool accent.

MAKES 20 TO 24 PIECES

1 pound asparagus, ends trimmed, cut into ¼-inch diagonal pieces
2 garlic cloves, minced
2 tablespoons extra virgin olive oil
¼ teaspoon salt
¼ cup water
Butter or extra virgin olive oil (optional)
Four 9- to 10-inch burrito-size tortillas, preferably from sprouted whole wheat,
    or 4 whole wheat tortillas
¼ cup Red Chile Paste
8 ounces (2 cups) grated sharp Cheddar, Gruyère, or Monterey Jack cheese,
    preferably raw

Place the asparagus, garlic, oil, salt, and water in a large skillet. Cover and cook 2 to 3 minutes over medium heat, until the asparagus is just tender. Uncover, raise the heat, and cook, stirring, until the liquid is evaporated and the asparagus is golden and caramelized, an additional 3 minutes or so. Transfer the asparagus to a bowl.

Spread the butter or brush the oil, if using, on one side of each tortilla and set the tortillas on a work surface, buttered side down. Spread a tablespoon of chile paste over the tortilla.

Distribute the cheese among the tortillas, covering only half of each and leaving a 1-inch margin at the edge. Distribute the asparagus on top of the cheese. Fold the tortillas in half to enclose the filling, creating a half-moon.

Put the quesadillas in a nonstick or cast-iron skillet over medium heat. Cook, covered, until the cheese melts and brown spots appear, about 4 minutes. Uncover and flip the quesadillas. Cook until the second side is golden brown and the cheese has melted completely, about 2 minutes.

Remove from the heat and divide each into 5 or 6 wedges.

Red Chile Paste

This spicy paste features two types of dried chiles and one type of fresh, which give the stuffed peppers and the asparagus quesadillas a remarkably complex flavor. It goes together quickly and can be prepared up to a month in advance.

MAKES ABOUT ½ CUP

¼ pound tomatillos (about 4 medium), husked and rinsed

1 small plum tomato

1 fresh serrano chile

2 dried pasilla chiles

5 dried chiles de arbol

2 garlic cloves, peeled, root ends trimmed but left whole

2 tablespoons water

½ teaspoon salt

⅛ teaspoon ground cumin

⅛ teaspoon ground cinnamon

Preheat the broiler. Place the tomatillos, tomato, and serrano chile on a broiler pan and place in the broiler for 6 to 8 minutes, turning, until all sides are blistered. When cool enough to handle, remove from the pan. Remove the stem and seeds of the chile. Transfer the tomatillos, tomato, and chile to a blender.

Slice off and remove the stem of the dried chiles and pour out the seeds. Heat a heavy-bottomed skillet, preferably cast iron, until very hot. Place the chiles in the skillet, in batches so you don't burn them, pressing down on them. Cook for a couple of seconds per side, until they blister and puff. Immediately remove the chiles and transfer to the blender. Cook the garlic for about 1 minute per side, until it starts to blacken. Transfer to the blender along with the water, salt, cumin, and cinnamon. Blend the paste until smooth, stopping to scrape down the sides.

Note: If your paste is more a watery purée (if your tomato or tomatillos were large) and makes about a cup, place the purée in a small pot on the stove. Cook, uncovered, stirring from time to time until it is thickened and no longer liquidy, 5 to 10 minutes. You should have about ½ cup. Transfer to a small jar.

Smoky Caesar Salad with Manchego and Pine Nuts

LEGEND HAS IT that Caesar salad was invented in Tijuana, Mexico, in 1924 by an Italian-American immigrant named Caesar Cardini. This delicious variation includes lime juice, manchego cheese, pine nuts, and a touch of smoked paprika. The dressing blends up quickly and keeps for a good week, refrigerated.

SERVES 6 (MAKES 1 CUP DRESSING)

3 garlic cloves, peeled and ends trimmed
2 anchovies packed in oil, drained
1 egg
½ teaspoon smoked paprika
2 tablespoons fresh lime juice
½ cup extra virgin olive oil
¾ teaspoon salt
Freshly ground black pepper
¼ cup plus ½ cup grated manchego cheese, preferably raw
1 head romaine, cut into bite-sized pieces (10 cups)
¼ cup pine nuts, toasted

Place the garlic, anchovies, egg, paprika, lime juice, olive oil, salt, and a sprinkling of black pepper in a blender and blend until smooth. Stir in ¼ cup of the cheese.

Place the romaine in a large salad bowl. Toss the dressing with the romaine. Divide onto plates. Serve, sprinkled with the pine nuts and the extra cheese.

VARIATIONS:

To make the dressing without the egg, add an additional tablespoon of the oil. You can also make the dressing without the anchovies for a vegetarian version.

Black Bean and Plantain–Stuffed Peppers

SWEET PLANTAINS and refried beans are baked into sweet red peppers for a festive side dish or a vegetarian main course. The tablespoon of chile paste makes all the difference. Serve these peppers with the tomatillo–pumpkinseed sauce (page 232).

The plantains need to be really ripe. The skin should be blackened in spots or all over and look like an overripe banana. Buy the ripe yellow ones a few days in advance and let them ripen even more.

For the cheese, you can use a good sharp Cheddar or Monterey Jack. Alternatively, try a Mexican cheese such as the mozzarella-like queso quesadilla, or a combination of queso quesadilla and firmer queso cotija.

SERVES 6

1½ cups black beans, soaked in water overnight
1 dried chipotle chile
Salt
6 large red bell peppers
2 tablespoons extra virgin olive oil, plus more for cooking the plantains
2 cups finely diced onions
3 garlic cloves, minced
2 teaspoons ground cumin
1 teaspoon dried oregano
1 tablespoon Red Chile Paste (page 229)
2 teaspoons fresh lime juice
3 ripe plantains
1½ cups grated Cheddar cheese, or queso quesadilla, or a mix of queso quesadilla with cotija, or Monterey Jack (optional)

Drain the beans and transfer to a medium pot. Add 4 cups of water and the chipotle chile, cover, and bring to a boil. Add 1¼ teaspoons salt, lower the heat, and simmer, partially covered, until the beans are tender, about 60 to 70 minutes. Check to make sure there is water to cover. Drain, reserving 1 cup of the cooking liquid, discarding the chile. (You can also pressure-cook the beans in 3 cups of water for 10 minutes.)

(continued)

Preheat the oven to 350°F. Cut the tops off the bell peppers and pull out and discard the seeds and membranes, keeping the peppers whole. Reserve the tops. Place the peppers on a baking dish and bake for 20 minutes, just until they start to soften.

Warm 2 tablespoons of the oil in a medium skillet. Add the onions and sauté over medium-low heat until softened, about 7 to 10 minutes. Add the garlic, cumin, and oregano and sauté an additional 3 minutes. Turn the heat up to medium. Add 1 cup of beans and ⅓ cup of the bean cooking liquid to the onions. With a potato masher or the back of a spoon, mash the beans into the liquid. Continue cooking until the liquid evaporates. Add another cup of the beans and ⅓ cup of the cooking liquid, and mash and cook again, stirring. Repeat one more time, adding the rest of the beans and ⅓ cup more cooking liquid, cooking and stirring, until the liquid is absorbed and the beans hold together. Some of the beans should be mashed and some will be whole. Stir in the chile paste and lime juice and adjust the salt to taste.

Cut the skins off the plantains. Use a paring knife, score the plantains and then peel back and remove the skins. Cut the plantains into ¼-inch diagonal pieces.

Film a large nonstick skillet with oil and heat over medium-high heat. Add half the plantain pieces, sprinkle with salt, and cook 2 to 3 minutes on each side, until golden brown. Repeat with a second batch, adding more oil if necessary. Stir into the beans.

Stir in ¾ cup of the cheese, if using, into the bean mixture, and stuff into the peppers. Distribute the remaining cheese on the top of the peppers. Position the reserved pepper tops back on the peppers. Transfer to a baking sheet and bake 30 minutes, until the peppers are completely softened and the cheese is melted.

Coconut-Cornmeal-Crusted Tilapia with Tomatillo-Pumpkin Mole

GOLDEN CORNMEAL-COCONUT–crusted fillets sit on top of a fresh green sauce. Serve this sauce with the stuffed peppers as well.

You can also make this with shrimp. Use 1½ pounds shrimp and sauté for 2 minutes on each side, until opaque. Finish for 1 minute in the oven.

SERVES 6 (MAKES 2 CUPS SAUCE)

Fish

I cup unsweetened coconut milk

1½ pounds tilapia (4 fillets, cut into 8 long pieces)

¾ cup cornmeal

¾ cup dried coconut

Salt and freshly ground black pepper

Sauce

½ pound tomatillos, papery husks removed, rinsed

I fresh serrano chile

I slice sourdough bread, 4 x 4 inches, ½ inch thick, crusts removed

I tablespoon extra virgin olive oil

I cup diced onion

2 garlic cloves, minced

½ cup pumpkinseeds, toasted

¾ cup water

¾ teaspoon salt

2 teaspoons lime juice

2 tablespoons chopped cilantro

Oil for sautéing, preferably coconut oil

Place the coconut milk in a shallow pan and soak the tilapia in it for at least 5 minutes.

In a shallow baking dish or on a plate, combine the cornmeal, coconut, ½ teaspoon salt, and a sprinkling of black pepper.

Remove the fish from the milk and press the fish into the coating, turning to press the coating onto both sides. Refrigerate the fish for at least 30 minutes to make the coating firmly adhere.

MAKE THE SAUCE: Preheat the broiler. Place the tomatillos and chile on a broiler pan and place in the broiler for 6 to 8 minutes, turning, until all sides are blistered. Remove from the pan. Remove the stem and seeds of the chile. Transfer the tomatillos and chile to a blender. Soak the bread in water to cover until softened, 2 to 3 minutes. Squeeze out the liquid and add the bread to the blender.

Meanwhile, warm the olive oil in a medium skillet. Add the onion and garlic and cook on medium-low heat until translucent, about 7 to 10 minutes. Transfer to the blender along with the pumpkinseeds, water, salt, lime juice, and cilantro. Blend until smooth.

(continued)

Taste and add additional salt if necessary. Transfer to a small pot and gently heat until warm.

COOK THE FISH: Remove the fish from the refrigerator and let come to room temperature. Preheat the oven to 400°F. Line a rimmed baking sheet with parchment or a Silpat.

Coat a large nonstick skillet with a thin layer of oil. Warm over medium-high heat until hot. (Test by holding your hand 1 inch above the skillet.) Lay half the fillets in the oil—they should sizzle—lower the heat, and cook until golden, about 3 to 4 minutes per side. Transfer the fillets to the baking sheet and repeat with the remaining fillets, adding more oil if necessary. Finish cooking the fish in the oven until the fish feels firm to the touch, about 3 to 5 minutes, depending on the thickness of the fish. Serve hot, on a pool of tomatillo sauce.

Coconut Crème Caramel with Roasted Banana–Chocolate Sauce

*H*ERE'S A SENSUOUS finish to your Cinco de Mayo fiesta. Bake the banana while the maple is caramelizing.

These can be made several days ahead. Two 8 x 8-inch Pyrex baking dishes will hold eight 1/2-cup ramekins.

MAKES EIGHT 4-OUNCE SERVINGS (MAKES 1 1/2 CUPS SAUCE)

Caramel
1/2 cup maple syrup

Custard
3 eggs, lightly beaten
1/2 cup sugar, preferably maple sugar or evaporated cane sugar
Pinch of salt
2 cups coconut milk
1 whole vanilla bean

Sauce

> 1 banana
>
> ¾ cup unsweetened coconut milk
>
> ¼ cup semisweet chocolate chips
>
> ¼ teaspoon vanilla extract
>
> 2 tablespoons maple syrup

Preheat the oven to 325°F. Pour 1 tablespoon of maple syrup into each of eight ½-cup ramekins or custard cups. Set the dishes into 1 or 2 larger baking dishes with sides. Place in the oven and bake for 30 minutes, or until the maple is bubbling.

MAKE THE CUSTARD: In a large bowl, combine the eggs, sugar, and salt.

Pour the coconut milk into a medium saucepan. Split the vanilla bean lengthwise down the center. Using the edge of a small knife or spoon, scrape the seeds out of the vanilla pod. Add the beans and pod to the milk. Heat the milk just below a boil, until scalded. Slowly whisk the hot milk into the egg mixture so as not to curdle the eggs.

Strain the mixture through a fine strainer into a large measuring cup or a pitcher.

Distribute the custard evenly among the ramekins. Have ready a kettle of hot water. Pull out the rack partway and set the baking dishes in the oven. Pour the hot water into the baking trays, reaching halfway up the sides of the custard dishes, making a hot water bath. Avoid splashing the custards.

Bake 35 to 40 minutes. To test for doneness, insert a thin-bladed knife between the center and the rim. The custard is done if the knife comes out clean. The center may not be completely set, but it will continue to cook in its own heat after removal from the oven. Remove the custard cups from the hot water bath and chill completely.

MAKE THE SAUCE: Place the whole unpeeled banana in the oven and bake until blackened and very soft, about 15 minutes. Cut the tip off at one end and squeeze the banana into a blender.

In a small saucepan, heat the coconut milk just until it reaches a boil. Turn off the heat and add the chocolate chips and cover. Let sit for 2 to 3 minutes. Uncover and add the vanilla and maple syrup and whisk until smooth. Add to the banana and blend until smooth. Reheat the sauce before serving.

Unmold the custards onto plates by running a knife around the edges. Drizzle a couple of tablespoons of warmed chocolate sauce around the custard.

Fourth of July

- Sunset Fruit Salad 240

- New Potato Salad with Sugar Snap Peas and Cherry Tomatoes 241

- Drunken Pinto Beans 242

- Grilled "Fireworks" Salad 243

- Grilled Tofu, Shrimp, and Chicken with Fourth of July Spice Rub 244

- Turkey Burger with Spicy Avocado Mustard 247

- Blueberry Buckle 248

ULY 4, THE ICONIC American holiday, commemorates the anniversary of the adoption of the Declaration of Independence. Americans perceive the holiday as a celebration of the birth of the United States and the political values that motivated the declaration itself, including equality and "certain unalienable rights . . . life, liberty, and the pursuit of happiness."

On June 11, 1776, the second Continental Congress, meeting in Philadelphia, appointed a committee of five to draft a document formally severing ties with the sovereign George III of England, explaining why the break was necessary. Thomas Paine, a master of rhetoric, had already primed the colonists for such a declaration in his widely distributed pamphlet *Common Sense*, published in January 1776. It stated among other things that colonists who shrank from a declaration of independence lacked not only common sense, but virtue and manhood. Jefferson crafted the first official draft, which went through a number of emendations. The declaration was ratified unanimously on July 2. After two more days of intense editing, the document as a finished piece was unanimously ratified on July 4. John Adams wrote to his wife Abigail on July 3, "I am apt to believe that it will be celebrated by succeeding generations as the great anniversary celebration . . . It ought to be solemnized with pomp and parade, with shows, games, sports, guns, bells, bonfires, and illuminations, from one end of the continent to the other, from this time forever more."

Adams's statement rang true. Ever since 1777, the midsummer holiday is marked by fireworks, patriotic displays, and outdoor events. The Fourth of July is often a day that construction of civic works begins and politicians speak. In the highest sense, it is a holiday that reminds us not to take liberty for granted. The meals usually gravitate around food that can be cooked outdoors and is easy to prepare for large groups of people.

In the spirit of independence, the feast presented here is eminently flexible, suitable for a picnic or a backyard grill gathering, depending on what you make. There's a "fireworks" salad with colorful grilled vegetables, made substantial and satisfying with the addition of spice-rubbed grilled chicken, tofu, and shrimp. Drunken beans can be made well in advance, and a potato, sugar snap pea, and tomato salad is dressed with lemon juice and olive oil. Sun-dried tomatoes and pine nuts stud grilled turkey burgers topped with an avocado-laced mustard. The Sunset Fruit Salad is lovely shades of red and orange summer fruit, and the Blueberry Buckle bursts with berries.

Cook's Notes

2 days before:

Make the Drunken Pinto Beans.
Make the grill rub.

Day before:

Make the Sunset Fruit Salad (except for the basil).
Make the Blueberry Buckle.
Make the marinade for the "fireworks" salad.
Form the turkey burgers.
Make the spice rub for the tofu, shrimp, and chicken. Rub the tofu, if using.

Day of:

Stir the basil into the fruit salad.
Make the new potato salad.
Marinate and grill the vegetables. Finish the "fireworks" salad.
Grill the turkey burgers.
Grill the tofu, shrimp, and chicken.
Rewarm the pinto beans.

Sunset Fruit Salad

*L*USCIOUS SEASONAL fruits in fiery reds and oranges are tossed with a raspberry reduction. Slivers of basil provide a bright and unusual accent.

SERVES 4 TO 6

1 cup raspberry-apple cider (or apple cider or apple juice)
½ cup red wine
1 tablespoon fresh lemon juice
½ cantaloupe, seeded and cut into 1-inch chunks
1 cup cherries, halved and pitted
1 cup strawberries, hulled and halved
1 cup raspberries
1 pound peaches, peeled and cut into chunks
10 basil leaves, cut into chiffonade (thin strands)

Pour the cider and wine into a small saucepan. Bring to a boil and cook, uncovered, until the liquid is reduced to ¼ cup, about 10 minutes. Remove from the heat and pour into a small bowl. Add the lemon juice to the reduced mixture and set aside to cool for a few minutes.

Put the cantaloupe, cherries, strawberries, raspberries, and peaches into a large bowl. Add the juice reduction and stir to combine. Refrigerate for at least 15 minutes to marry the flavors. Just before serving, gently stir in the basil.

New Potato Salad with Sugar Snap Peas and Cherry Tomatoes

THIS ATTRACTIVE salad is dressed with a lemony oregano-caper vinaigrette. For best results, make sure to use a low-starch potato, such as baby reds or white creamers. You can substitute delicate haricots verts for the sugar snap peas.

SERVES 4

1 pound small thin-skinned potatoes
Salt
½ pound sugar snap peas
1 cup cherry tomatoes, halved
2 teaspoons drained capers
2 tablespoons chopped fresh oregano
2 garlic cloves, minced
2 tablespoons fresh lemon juice
2 tablespoons extra virgin olive oil
Freshly ground black pepper

Cut the unpeeled potatoes into even chunks, about 1 inch on a side. You can keep the small ones whole.

Put the potatoes in a medium pot and add enough water to cover them by 1 inch. Bring to a boil, covered. Uncover, add 1 teaspoon of salt, and simmer just until the potatoes are tender, about 10 minutes.

Remove the potatoes from the water with a skimmer or slotted spoon and place in a medium bowl.

Return the water to a boil and add the peas. Cook until barely tender, approximately 1 minute. Drain and transfer to a bowl filled with cold or ice water to stop the cooking.

Drain the peas and add to the potatoes, along with the tomatoes, capers, oregano, and garlic.

In a small bowl, whisk together the lemon juice, olive oil, 1 teaspoon salt, and a sprinkling of black pepper. Mix into the vegetables and gently stir to combine. Add more salt and pepper if necessary. Serve at room temperature.

Drunken Pinto Beans

THIS SPICY party dish is cooked with beer and finished with tequila. All of the alcohol cooks out, leaving the saucy beans with a deep, rich flavor, tasting as if they've been baked for hours. It's a great dish to make ahead and reheat.

SERVES 6

1½ cups pinto beans, soaked overnight or hot-soaked (see page 11)
One 12-ounce bottle of beer
1 tablespoon ground cumin
1 dried chipotle chile
Salt
2 tablespoons extra virgin olive oil
1 small onion, cut into small dice (½ cup)
3 garlic cloves, minced
3 tomatoes, peeled, seeded, and diced (1 cup)
1 jalapeño pepper, stemmed, seeded, and minced
1 teaspoon dried oregano
⅓ cup tequila
1 tablespoon fresh lime juice

Drain the pinto beans and mix them with the beer, cumin, chile, and 3 cups of water in a medium pot or saucepan. Cover and bring to a boil. Lower the heat, stir in 1¼ teaspoons salt, and simmer, partially covered, until the beans are tender, about 1 to 1½ hours. Check from time to time, making sure there is enough water to cover the beans.

When the beans are almost tender, warm the olive oil in a medium skillet. Add the onion and garlic and sauté over medium heat until softened, about 7 minutes. Add the tomatoes, jalapeño, oregano, and tequila, and cook for about 10 minutes, until the tomatoes are softened and the tequila has evaporated. Add to the beans and simmer 15 minutes, uncovered, to marry the flavors and thicken. Remove and discard the chipotle chile. Stir in the lime juice. Taste and add more salt if necessary. Serve hot.

Grilled "Fireworks" Salad

THIS IS the perfect salad for sultry summer evenings. Grilled zucchini, corn, red onion, and red bell pepper are combined with spinach and tomatoes and dressed with a warm herbed vinaigrette. For a light main course, top the salad with Grilled Tofu, Shrimp, and Chicken with Fourth of July Spice Rub.

Grilled portobello mushrooms and asparagus are good additions. The leftovers taste great in frittatas, quiches, or tofu scrambles.

SERVES 4 TO 6 AS A MAIN-COURSE SALAD

1 pound zucchini (3 small or 2 medium)

2 ears corn

1 medium red onion

1 large red bell pepper

12 cups spinach (from 1½ pounds, stemmed, or ¾ pound baby), washed and dried

1 cup cherry tomatoes, halved

6 tablespoons balsamic vinegar

6 tablespoons extra virgin olive oil

¼ cup chopped fresh parsley

¼ cup chopped fresh basil

3 garlic cloves, minced

Salt and freshly ground black pepper

Grilled Tofu, Shrimp, and Chicken with Fourth of July Spice Rub (optional)
(recipe follows)

Preheat a grill or a grill pan on medium heat.

Cut the stems off the zucchini and discard. Slice the zucchini into ½-inch lengthwise slabs. Husk the corn and remove the silk. Peel and cut the onion into ½-inch rings. Cut the bell pepper into flat pieces or one large flat slab.

Place the zucchini, corn, onion, and bell pepper in a shallow baking dish. Place the spinach and tomatoes in a large bowl.

In a small bowl, whisk together the vinegar, oil, parsley, basil, garlic, 1 teaspoon salt,

(continued)

and a sprinkling of black pepper. Pour into the shallow baking dish, using tongs to turn. Make sure every vegetable is moistened by the marinade. You may need to remove some to a plate to make room to coat all the vegetables. You can grill the vegetables right away or leave them in the marinade for up to 30 minutes.

Grill the zucchini, onion, and bell pepper until tender and marked with grill marks, about 3 minutes per side. Grill the corn about 5 minutes total, turning frequently so that all sides touch the grill. Remove the zucchini, onion, and bell pepper to a cutting board and cut them into bite-size pieces. Cut the kernels off the cobs and add to the spinach and tomatoes.

Pour the remaining marinade into a small saucepan and heat just until it reaches a boil. Pour the marinade over the vegetables, sprinkle with salt and pepper, and toss to combine. Toss or top with the grilled tofu, shrimp, and chicken, if using. Serve warm or at room temperature.

Grilled Tofu, Shrimp, and Chicken with Fourth of July Spice Rub

THE TOFU can be brushed with oil and the spice rub for up to 24 hours in advance. The spice rub slipped under the shrimp shell permeates the shrimp with flavor and the shrimp is grilled shell on, to achieve the perfect texture. The chicken is butterflied to cook quickly on the grill, so that it stays moist.

Grill one or a combination of these and serve on top of the grilled "fireworks" salad for a splendid main-course entrée. Extra spice rub can be stored in a covered jar for up to 2 months.

SERVES 4 TO 6 (MAKES 9 TABLESPOONS SPICE RUB)

Spice Rub

I tablespoon cumin seed

I tablespoon coriander seed

I tablespoon fennel seed

2 tablespoons paprika

I tablespoon black peppercorns

I tablespoon salt

I tablespoon sugar, preferably a natural one such as maple sugar

I tablespoon dried oregano

Tofu

I pound firm or extra firm tofu

3 tablespoons spice rub

3 tablespoons extra virgin olive oil, plus more for brushing

Shrimp

2 tablespoons spice rub

2 tablespoons extra virgin olive oil

½ pound large shrimp (**9 to 12**)

Chicken

2 tablespoons extra virgin olive oil

2 tablespoons spice rub

3 boneless chicken breasts

MAKE THE SPICE RUB: Place all the ingredients in a spice grinder and grind until powdered.

MAKE THE TOFU: Press the tofu between 2 pie plates for about 30 minutes to remove the excess water. Lay the tofu on its side and cut into 4 slices lengthwise. In a small bowl, mix the spice rub with the olive oil. Use a brush to apply the rub onto all sides of the tofu. Place the slabs back into a block and wrap it in plastic. Store in the refrigerator for at least an hour and up to 24 hours to absorb the spices.

Heat an outdoor grill or a grill pan to medium-high. Brush the tofu on one side with oil. Grill, oil side down, about 2 to 3 minutes, rotating the tofu on an angle halfway through

(continued)

to get crosshatched grill marks. Oil the second side and flip and repeat. Cut into pieces or leave as "steaks."

MAKE THE SHRIMP: Mix the spice rub with the olive oil.

Using kitchen shears, cut through the back of the shells to expose the vein. Pull out the veins with a toothpick if necessary. Peel back the shells without pulling them off. Brush the rub under the shells, folding the shells back in place. String the shrimp along a double skewer to make it easy to turn them.

Preheat the grill to medium-high. Grill the shrimp 5 minutes per side. Peel off the shells before tossing in the salad.

MAKE THE CHICKEN: Combine the oil and spice rub. Slice the chicken breasts through the middle to make 6 cutlets (see illustration below). Brush each side with the spice mixture. Preheat the grill to medium-high. Grill on one side until the chicken has marks, about 2 to 3 minutes. Turn and continue to grill (uncovered for charcoal, covered for gas) until the chicken is just firm to the touch and just cooked through, 3 to 4 minutes. If you are using a grill pan, use a dome lid to cover the chicken. Transfer to a serving platter and let rest for 5 minutes. Cut into pieces or leave whole and serve on top of the salad.

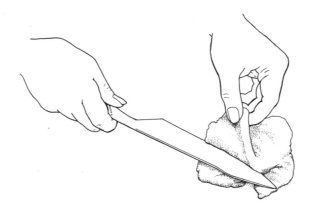

Turkey Burger with Spicy Avocado Mustard

THESE WELL-SEASONED patties are laced with sun-dried tomatoes and pine nuts. Sautéed onions and bell peppers keep them moist, even when grilled. Serve with or without buns, topped with a dollop of the avocado mustard.

MAKES 6 BURGERS

2 tablespoons extra virgin olive oil

1 cup onion, diced small

2 garlic cloves, minced

1 green bell pepper, cut into small dice

1 teaspoon ground cumin

1 teaspoon chili powder

1 jalapeño pepper, stemmed, seeded, and minced

1 pound ground turkey

¼ cup sun-dried tomatoes (not in oil) (about 7), reconstituted and
    chopped into ¼ inch dice (see Note)

¼ cup pine nuts, lightly toasted

½ teaspoon salt

Freshly ground black pepper

1 egg white

Spicy Avocado Mustard

1 ripe avocado, preferably Hass

4 teaspoons fresh lime juice

4 teaspoons Dijon mustard

1 jalapeño pepper, stemmed, seeded, and minced

Warm the oil in a medium skillet. Add the onion, garlic, and bell pepper, and sauté over medium heat until softened, about 7 to 10 minutes. Add the cumin, chili powder, and jalapeño, and sauté another 3 minutes.

Transfer to a medium bowl and stir in the turkey, tomatoes, pine nuts, salt, and a sprin-

(continued)

kling of black pepper. Stir in the egg white and form into 6 burgers. Refrigerate for an hour or longer.

Heat an outdoor grill or a grill pan to medium. Add the burgers and cook 4 minutes on each side, crosshatching after 2 minutes to get pronounced grill marks. Cover and cook another 4 minutes or so on low heat (if using a grill pan, put a domed lid over the burgers until they are cooked through). They will feel firm when pressed.

MAKE THE AVOCADO MUSTARD: Scoop the flesh of the avocado into a bowl. Add the lime juice, mustard, and jalapeño and mash until well combined.

Note: Pour hot water over the tomatoes and let sit for 10 minutes to soften.

Blueberry Buckle

*T*HIS MOIST streusel-topped cake bursts with juicy berries. The batter is thick, like a cookie dough, to support the weight of the berries. Use a springform pan and be sure to use fresh blueberries.

Some natural sugars are moister than others. The streusel will take 4 to 6 tablespoons of melted butter or oil, depending on the type of sugar you use.

MAKES ONE 9-INCH CAKE

Streusel

¾ cup whole wheat pastry flour

½ cup pecans

⅓ cup granulated sugar, preferably a natural one such as maple, evaporated
    cane sugar, or Demerara

1 teaspoon ground cinnamon

½ teaspoon baking powder

Pinch of salt

4 to 6 tablespoons butter, melted, or melted coconut oil
    (canola oil may be substituted)

Cake

I cup whole wheat pastry flour

I cup unbleached white flour

2 teaspoons baking powder

$\frac{1}{3}$ cup melted coconut oil or melted butter (canola oil may be substituted)

$\frac{3}{4}$ cup maple syrup

2 teaspoons vanilla extract

$\frac{1}{2}$ teaspoon salt

4 cups fresh blueberries

MAKE THE STREUSEL: In a food processor, pulse the flour, pecans, and sugar until you have a coarse meal. Transfer to a bowl and add the cinnamon, baking powder, and salt, and mix well. Slowly drizzle in the oil, adding the oil a tablespoon at a time, tossing with your fingers until the mixture is moistened. The mixture should be the consistency of wet sand, with pebbles ranging in size from crumbs to larger pebbles. If after 6 tablespoons of oil the mixture looks dry, add a few drops of water to get it to the right texture. Set aside.

MAKE THE CAKE: Oil a 9-inch springform pan and set aside. Preheat the oven to 350°F.

Sift the flours and baking powder into a medium bowl. Stir to blend. In a second bowl, whisk the oil, maple syrup, vanilla, and salt until thoroughly blended.

Pour the wet ingredients into the flour mixture and mix with a rubber spatula until the dry ingredients are completely moistened. The batter will be very thick.

Stir the blueberries into the batter.

Spread the batter into the cake pan. Sprinkle the streusel on top to cover the cake. Bake on the center rack of the oven until a toothpick inserted in the center comes out dry and the sides pull away from the pan, about 70 minutes. If the cake starts to darken too much but the inside is not completely cooked, tent the top with foil. Remove from the oven and set on a rack to cool for 30 minutes. Remove from the pan and let cool completely before serving.

Resources

BOBSREDMILL.COM

Great selection of grains and flours, including teff flour.

BRIDGE KITCHENWARE
214 East 52nd Street
New York, NY 10022
212-838-1901, ext. #3 (in New York)
Info and customer service 212-838-6746, ext. #5
Fax: 212-758-5387
Catalogue orders only
800-BRIDGE K (800-274-3435), ext. #3
www.bridgekitchenware.com

Excellent selection of kitchen tools. Extensive online catalogue.

CHEF'S CATALOGUE
3215 Commercial Avenue
Northbrook, IL 60062
800-338-3232
www.chefscatalog.com

Good equipment resource, wonderful online catalogue, All-Clad pots and pans.

COOMBS FAMILY FARMS
P.O. Box 117
Brattleboro, VT 05302
888-266-6271
www.coombsfamilyfarms.com

Excellent source for high-quality maple sugar, from 1- to 40-pound packages, and maple syrup. They own their own sugarhouse. Maple powder is the finest grind.

COYOTE CAFE GENERAL STORE
132 West Water Street
Santa Fe, NM 87501
505-982-2454
800-866-HOWL (4695)

Chiles. Mail-order catalogue.

DIAMOND ORGANICS
Highway 1
Moss Landing, CA 95039
888-ORGANIC (674-2642)
Fax 888-888-6777
www.diamondorganics.com
e-mail: info@diamondorganics.com

Farm-fresh organic food, including vegetables and meat, with guaranteed overnight deliveries.

FILLO FACTORY
P.O. Box 155
Dumont, NJ 07628
800-653-4556 (800-OK-FILLO)
www.fillofactory.com

Best commercial phyllo available. Available in stores around the country. You can check their Web site to see which stores in each state carry them. They also ship directly.

GOLDMINE NATURAL FOOD COMPANY
7805 Arjons Drive
San Diego, CA 92126-4368
800-475-FOOD (3663)
www.goldminenaturalfood.com

Amazing selection of the highest-quality organic grains, including brown and golden teff, dried chestnuts, organic dried fruit, hard-to-find products, beans, sea vegetables, varieties of high-quality sea salt, and condiments. They ship within 24 hours; orders take just a couple of days in the United States, about 1 week internationally.

THE GRAIN AND SALT SOCIETY
P.O. Box 19502
273 Fairway Drive
Asheville, NC 28805
800-867-7258
www.celtic-seasalt.com

Great resource for Celtic sea salt and accessories.

J. B. PRINCE COMPANY, INC.
36 East 31st Street
New York, NY 10016
212-683-3553
Fax: 212-683-4488

Large selection of baking supplies. Mail order.

KALUSTYAN'S
123 Lexington Avenue
New York, NY 10016
212-685-3451
www.Kalustyans.com

Top on my list of places to visit in New York. Huge selection of spices, condiments from all over the world. Best place to get exotic ingredients, including fermented black beans, chiles, spices, beans and grains of every type, berbere powder, smoked paprika, rose and orange blossom waters, Szechuan peppercorns. Mail order available.

NEW YORK CAKE AND BAKING DISTRIBUTOR
56 West 22nd Street
New York, NY 10010
212-675-CAKE (2253)
800-942-2539
NYcake.com

Large selection of baking supplies, aluminum ramekins. Mail order.

OMEGA NUTRITION
6515 Aldrich Road
Bellingham, WA 98226
800-661-3529
www.omeganutrition.com
Info@omeganutrition.com
Order online: omegahealthstore.com

Superior organic oils, including my favorite all-purpose filtered coconut oil. Excellent virgin coconut oil also. They ship quickly.

PENZEY'S SPICES
262-785-7676
800-741-7787
Fax: 262-785-7678
www.penzeys.com

Mail-order spice catalogue. Thirty-four retail stores. Excellent quality and selection. 250 spices and spice blends, including dried chiles and vanilla beans.

POSEIDON BAKERY
629 Ninth Avenue (between 44th and 45th streets)
New York, NY 10036
212-757-6173

A wonderful place to visit in New York. The best-quality handmade fresh phyllo. No mail order.

SAHADI IMPORTING COMPANY
187 Atlantic Avenue
Brooklyn, NY 11201-5696
718-624-4550

Middle Eastern ingredients.

TIENDA.COM

Smoked paprika.

WESTON A. PRICE FOUNDATION
4200 Wisconsin Avenue, NW
Washington, DC 20016
202-333-HEAL (4325)
www.WestonAPrice.org
www.pricepottenger.org

Foundation based on the research of nutrition pioneer Dr. Weston Price. This organization is a clearinghouse of information on healthful lifestyles, ecology, sound nutrition, alternative medicine, humane farming, and organic gardening.

Fascinating, informative Web site with lots of links, including realmilk.com, which lists folks to contact about purchasing raw milk directly from the farmer. It includes each state, area by area.

WILDERNESS FAMILY NATURALS
P.O. Box 538
Finland, MN 55603
Orders toll free: 866-936-6457
Questions: 800-945-3801
www.wildernessfamilynaturals.com

Delicious virgin coconut oil and expeller pressed coconut oil, suitable for high-heat cooking.

WORLDSPICE.COM

Wonderful selection of spices and spice blends, including smoked paprika, five-spice powder, and fenugreek.

Glossary of Ingredients

ANCHO CHILE: Dried poblano, the most commonly used chile in Mexico. The sweetest of the dried chiles, it has a mild fruit flavor. The name means "wide" in Spanish, and it measures 4 to 5 inches long and 3 inches across and has a dark mahogany color.

BROWN RICE VINEGAR: Traditionally brewed vinegar imported from Japan made from rice, koji, and spring water. Smooth and mellow flavor with low acidity.

CHILE DE ARBOL: Tiny, dried "treelike" chiles. Closely related to cayenne with a searing, acidic heat. Bright red, about 2 to 3 inches long and $^1/_2$ inch wide.

CHINESE BLACK BEANS: Black soybeans that have been fermented. They give a distinctive flavor to Chinese black bean sauces. They are sold in Asian markets and gourmet stores and they keep indefinitely. A quick couple of rinses removes the excess salt.

CHIPOTLE CHILES: Smoked jalapeño chile peppers with a hot, smoky, sweet flavor. These chiles are usually a dull tan to coffee color and measure approximately 2 to 4 inches in length and about an inch wide.

CHIPOTLE CHILES IN ADOBO SAUCE: Smoked jalapeños, these come packed in small cans in a tomato-based sauce, convenient to use. You can store the rest in a jar in the refrigerator for many months. They are readily available in gourmet markets and natural foods stores.

GUAJILLO CHILE: Shiny, deep orange-red-brown dried chile. Measures 4 to 6 inches long, tapering to a point. Medium heat level with an uncomplicated taste, a little citrus and tart.

HACHIYA PERSIMMONS: Acorn-shaped, with pointy ends; much brighter orange than the squatter Fuyu variety. They are sold hard in the stores and you have to leave them out on the counter to ripen, a process known as bletting. They soften up, and the softer they get, the better they taste. They are ready to eat when they have the consistency of a water balloon. Ripe hachiyas have a rich, honeylike flavor.

INDIAN RED CHILES: Similar to cayenne peppers, these are the chiles in Indian chili powder.

MAPLE SUGAR: Crystallized maple syrup.

MISO: Fermented soy paste, made by mixing cooked soybeans with koji, salt, and water and fermenting the mixture from 2 months to 3 years. Used to make soup and as an addition to many different dishes. High in protein and loaded with enzymes that help digestion. Huge variety of misos ranges from mild and light to full-bodied and dark.

NEW MEXICAN CHILE: Scarlet, elongated, tapered chile measuring 5 to 7 inches long and 1½ to 2 inches across. It has an uncomplicated red chile flavor. Sold in the form of crushed flakes and ground powders; also known as chile colorado.

ORANGE BLOSSOM WATER: In the United States Lebanese versions are available in Middle Eastern stores and the French version is often available in gourmet markets and stores that sell baking supplies.

PASILLA CHILES: Dark raisin brown dried chiles measuring 5 to 6 inches long and 1½ inches across. It ranges from medium to medium hot. It literally means "little raisin" and is also known as chile negro.

POMEGRANATE SYRUP: Also known as **pomegranate molasses** or **concentrated pomegranate juice**, this thick deliciously sweet-tart syrup is made from reducing pomegranate juice. It is used frequently in Turkish and Iranian cooking. You can find it in gourmet markets and Middle Eastern groceries.

RICE SYRUP: Mild sweetener with a subtle butterscotch flavor made from rice. Good for savory foods as well as desserts, or for those who barely want any sweetener.

ROSE WATER: Distilled roses in water. An important flavoring in Middle Eastern food. Buy it in gourmet groceries, natural foods stores, and Middle Eastern groceries.

SHOYU: Traditionally aged soy sauce. The only ingredients in it should be soy, wheat, water, and salt. The traditional method of making soy sauce ensures that it has a bright fresh taste. It is readily available in natural foods markets, gourmet markets, Asian markets, and many supermarkets.

SMOKED PAPRIKA: The name given to the sweet and slightly hot members of the capsicum family that are naturally wood smoked before grinding, giving them a robust aroma and flavor.

TAPIOCA: Comes from the roots of the cassava plant. It is available as tapioca or cassava flour or as pearled tapioca, which undergoes a "beading" process that gives the pearls a pebbly texture desirable in puddings.

Equivalency Tables

Common Measurements

VOLUME TO VOLUME

3 tsp = 1 tbsp

4 tbsp = ¼ cup

5⅓ tbsp = ⅓ cup

4 ounces = ½ cup

8 ounces = 1 cup

1 cup = ½ pint

VOLUME TO WEIGHT

¼ cup liquid or fat = 2 ounces

½ cup liquid or fat = 4 ounces

1 cup liquid or fat = 8 ounces

2 cups liquid or fat = 1 pound

1 cup sugar = 7 ounces

1 cup flour = 5 ounces

Metric Equivalencies
(Liquid and Dry Measure Equivalencies)

CUSTOMARY	METRIC
¼ teaspoon	1.25 milliliters
½ teaspoon	2.5 milliliters
1 teaspoon	5 milliliters
1 tablespoon	15 milliliters
1 fluid ounce	30 milliliters
¼ cup	60 milliliters
⅓ cup	80 milliliters
½ cup	120 milliliters
1 cup	240 milliliters
1 pint (2 cups)	480 milliliters
1 quart (4 cups)	960 milliliters (.96 liter)
1 gallon (4 quarts)	3.84 liters
1 ounce (by weight)	28 grams
¼ pound (4 ounces)	114 grams
1 pound (16 ounces)	454 grams
2.2 pounds	1 kilogram (1,000 grams)

Oven–Temperature Equivalencies

DESCRIPTION	°FAHRENHEIT	°CELSIUS
Cool	200	90
Very slow	250	120
Slow	300–325	150–160
Moderately slow	325–350	160–180
Moderate	350–375	180–190
Moderately hot	375–400	190–200
Hot	400–450	200–230
Very hot	450–500	230–260

Index

About the Author

MYRA KORNFELD is the author of *The Healthy Hedonist* and *The Voluptuous Vegan.* She teaches at the Natural Gourmet Institute for Food and Health as well as the Institute of Culinary Education in New York City. A veteran restaurant chef and *Vegetarian Times* contributor, she specializes in cooking parties and corporate team-building events. Visit her at www .myrakornfeld.com.